CW00517262

Turboprops: Low- High-Performance

When I hear the term turboprop, my mind immediately, rightly, or wrongly, thinks of the Beechcraft King Air. This American twin first appeared in the early 1970s. Today the production line in Wichita has rolled-out nearly 7,500 aircraft that were delivered to commercial, private, para-public, government and military customers around the world. The King Air is a great looking aircraft with commendable performance. King Air aircraft operate in nations around the world, many very much in the public gaze.

But the King Air is a utility aircraft and just one of a variety of turboprop types in service, from light general aviation designs through commuter aircraft and trainer aircraft to ATR and Q400 airliners and the A400M Atlas heavy transport, each one is defined as a turboprop. By definition, a turboprop refers to an aircraft equipped with a turbine engine, a propellor and a gear box. Almost all the engine's power is used to drive the propeller through a coupled reduction gear

that converts the high RPM, low torque output to low RPM, high torque. In general, the propeller spins at a constant speed with variable pitch.

Most types featured in this edition are in production, and four chapters focus on turboprop operators: the Luftwaffe A400 Atlas, the Força Aerea Portuguesa C295, the Schweize Luftwaffe PC-21 trainer, and the British Antarctica Survey Twin Otter and Dash 8.

Turboprops: Low-cost, High-performance should answer every question you ever had about the world's leading turboprop aircraft.

Mark Ayton

Mark Ayton
Editor

IMAGE • *Textron Aviation*

CONTENTS

CREDIT: PILATUS

CREDIT: DE HAVILLAND CANADA

MAIN COVER IMAGE: BEECHCRAFT

CREDIT: AIRBUS

CREDIT: PIPER

Contents

ISBN: 978 1 80282 637 1
Editor: Mark Ayton
Senior editor, specials: Roger Mortimer
Email: roger.mortimer@keypublishing.com
Cover Design: Dan Hilliard
Design: PA Media
Advertising Sales Manager: Brodie Baxter
Email: brodie.baxter@keypublishing.com
Tel: 01780 755131
Advertising Production: Debi McGowan
Email: debi.mcgowan@keypublishing.com

SUBSCRIPTION/MAIL ORDER
Key Publishing Ltd, PO Box 300, Stamford, Lincs, PE9 1NA
Tel: 01780 480404
Subscriptions email: subs@keypublishing.com
Mail Order email: orders@keypublishing.com
Website: www.keypublishing.com/shop

PUBLISHING
Group CEO: Adrian Cox
Publisher: Jonathan Jackson
Published by: Key Publishing Ltd, PO Box 100, Stamford, Lincs, PE9 1XP
Tel: 01780 755131 **Website:** www.keypublishing.com

PRINTING
Precision Colour Printing Ltd, Haldane,
Halesfield 1, Telford, Shropshire. TF7 4QQ

DISTRIBUTION
Seymour Distribution Ltd, 2 Poultry Avenue, London, EC1A 9PU
Enquiries Line: 02074 294000.

We are unable to guarantee the bonafides of any of our advertisers. Readers are strongly recommended to take their own precautions before parting with any information or item of value, including, but not limited to money, manuscripts, photographs, or personal information in response to any advertisements within this publication.

© Key Publishing Ltd 2023
All rights reserved. No part of this magazine may be reproduced or transmitted in any form by any means, electronic or mechanical, including photocopying, recording or by any information storage and retrieval system, without prior permission in writing from the copyright owner. Multiple copying of the contents of the magazine without prior written approval is not permitted.

KEY
Publishing

Turboprops: An Insight

An overview of the turboprop, a dip into its history and the most popular engine type

ABOVE • *Vickers Viscount prototype, registration G-AHRF flying in BEA colours for promotional purposes. The Viscount was powered by four Rolls-Royce Dart turboprop engines.*
BAE SYSTEMS

Many aircraft use turboprop propulsion comprising a gas turbine, a gearbox, and a propeller.

Thrust is generated by moving a large mass of air through a small change in velocity. The turboprop's gas turbine core expands all the hot exhaust through the nozzle to produce thrust, most of the energy of the exhaust is used to turn the turbine.

An additional turbine stage is connected to a drive shaft which is connected to a gear box and then connected to a propeller that produces most of the thrust.

A turboprop's exhaust velocity is low and contributes little thrust because most of the energy of the core exhaust has gone into turning the drive shaft.

Turboprops are used for low-speed aircraft because propellers become less efficient as the speed of the aircraft increases, but offer advantages in reliability, efficiency, and versatility.

Despite the efforts by Hungarian physicist and engineer György Jendrassik in 1939, turboprops were not used to power aircraft until the late 1940s. British OEM Vickers selected the Rolls-Royce Dart turboprop to power its Viscount, a four-engine commercial airliner with a pressurised cabin, capable of carrying up to 65 passengers.

The Vickers Viscount offered a smoother flight with less noise and vibration than its piston engine powered contemporaries and from an operator's perspective, it did it with lower operating costs.

On the other side of the Atlantic, Lockheed launched the first American turboprop airliner in the shape of the L-188 Electra. Its launch customer was American Airlines.

Turboprops provide short take-off and landing capability which makes the aircraft ideal for operating in and out of remote, austere airfields and unimproved strips.

NASA's Advanced Turboprop Project

In its brief write-up of the Advanced Turboprop project, the National Aeronautics and Space Administration (NASA) says: *"In 1987, a Washington Post headline read, 'The aircraft engine of the future has propellers on it'. To many this statement was something like heralding 'the reincarnation of silent movies'. Why would an 'old technology' ever be chosen over a modern, new, advanced alternative? How could propeller technology ever supplant the turbojet revolution? How could the 'Jet set mind-set' of corporate executives, who demanded the prestige of speed and 'image and status with a jet', ever be satisfied with a slow, noisy, propeller-driven aircraft?*

"A Washington Times correspondent predicted that the turbojet would not be the propulsion system of the future. Instead, the future would witness more propellers than jets and if 'Star Wars hero Luke Skywalker ever became chairman of a Fortune 500 company, he would replace the corporate jet with a … turboprop'. It appeared that a turboprop revolution was underway.

"NASA Lewis Research Center's Advanced Turboprop Project (1976-1987) was the source of this optimism. The energy crisis of the early 1970s served

LEFT • *Pratt & Whitney Canada's PT6A turboprop engine.* PRATT & WHITNEY CANADA

BELOW • *An advanced propeller swirl recovery model in the NASA Lewis Research Center's 8ft x 6ft supersonic wind tunnel. It aimed to provide the technology base to enable development of quieter, fuel efficient, turboprop engines.* NASA

as the catalyst for renewed government interest in aeronautics and NASA launched this ambitious project to return to fuel saving, propeller-driven aircraft.

"The Arab oil embargo brought difficult times to all of America, but the airlines industry suffered and feared for its future in the wake of a steep rise in fuel prices.

"NASA responded to these fears by creating a programme to improve aircraft fuel efficiency. Of the six projects NASA funded through this programme, the Advanced Turboprop Project promised the greatest payoffs in terms of fuel savings, but it was also the most conceptually radical and technically demanding.

"The project began in the early 1970s with the collaboration of two engineers, Daniel Mikkelson from NASA Lewis, and Carl Rohrbach of Hamilton Standard, the nation's last majoar propeller manufacturer. Mikkelson, then a young aeronautical research engineer, went back to the old National Advisory Committee for Aeronautics (NACA) wind tunnel reports where he found a 'glimmer of hope' that propellers could be designed to make propeller-powered aircraft fly faster and higher than those of the mid to late-1950s.

"Mikkelson and Rohrbach came up with the concept of sweeping the propeller blades to reduce noise and increase efficiency and NASA received a joint patent with Hamilton Standard for the development of this technology.

"At Lewis, Mikkelson sparked the interest of a small cadre of engineers and managers. They solved key technical problems essential for the creation of the turboprop, while at the

same time they attracted support for the project. After a project office was established, they became political advocates, using technical gains and increasing acceptance to fight for continued funding. This involved winning government, industry, and public support for the new propellor technology.

"Initially the project involved only Hamilton Standard, but the aircraft engine manufacturers, Pratt & Whitney, Allison, and General Electric, and the giants of the airframe industry, Boeing, Lockheed, and McDonnell Douglas joined the bandwagon as the turboprop appeared to become more and more technically and socially feasible. The turboprop project became a large, well-funded, 'heterogeneous collection of human and material resources' that contemporary historians refer to as 'big science'. At its height it involved over 40 industrial contracts, 15 university grants, and work at the four NASA research centers, Lewis, Langley, Dryden, and Ames. The progress of the advanced turboprop development seemed to foreshadow its future dominance of commercial flight...

"Despite this technical success, the predicted turboprop revolution never came, and no commercial or military air fleet replaced jets with propellers."

Pratt & Whitney Canada's PT6A

Despite a lack of take-up of the American advanced turboprop project, the turboprop concept was already well-established, not least with Pratt & Whitney Canada. Since May 30, 1961, the date of the first flight, the company's

PT6 has and continues to power thousands of single- and twin-engine aircraft around the world. Over 55,000 PT6 engines have been produced to date.

According to Pratt & Whitney Canada: "The PT6's flexible engine architecture and modular reverse flow design simplifies installation in both single- and twin-engine installations as well as tractor and pusher propeller configurations. Simple, on-wing maintenance is possible for most tasks, where other engines might need a shop visit.

"The PT6A configuration has proven to be a key attribute to its success: its rearward, reverse flow inlet and forward-facing turbine section provide fast maintenance turn-around through on-wing hot section refurbishment in most aircraft installations."

The PT6A is a two-shaft engine with a multi-stage compressor driven by a single-stage compressor turbine and an independent shaft coupling the power turbine to the propeller through an epicyclic concentric reduction gearbox.

The Canadian company details the main components thus:

- Multi-stage axial and single-stage centrifugal compressor provides reverse flow and has a radial inlet with a screen for foreign object damage protection.
- Reverse-flow combustor creates low-levels of emissions, and provides high stability, and easy starting.
- Single-stage compressor turbine features cooled vanes in some models to maintain high durability.
- Independent free power turbine with shrouded blades provides forward-facing output for fast refurbishment of the hot section.
- Epicyclic speed reduction gearbox enables compact installation and an optimised output speed that generates the highest power and low propeller noise.
- Electronic engine control on many models provides ease of operation and reduced pilot workload.

The manufacturers state that the PT6A is the only engine with single engine instrument flight rules status for passenger revenue activity in Australia, Europe, New Zealand, and North America. Seventy models are available that offer flexibility and capability for a variety of applications. The PT6 engine family currently powers aircraft in service with over 7,100 operators in more than 180 countries, with an accumulated 400+ million flying hours to date.

Europe's Problem Child

A report by Frank Visser and Ludo Mennes on A400M operations with Lufttransportgeschwader 62 based at Wunstorf Air Base, Germany

ABOVE • *Parachutists jump from the aft cargo door of A400M test aircraft registration F-WWMS (msn 003).*
AIRBUS

Germany originally ordered 53 A400M Atlas aircraft to replace its fleet of two-engine Transall C-160Ds, the last of which was retired in December 2021. The Luftwaffe had planned to accept just 40 to save money, but the sale of the 13 aircraft was not realised,

neither could a planned international A400 squadron based at Lechfeld Air Base located south of the city of Augsburg.

Challenges
Introducing a new aircraft to an air force is rarely a walk in the park. Too

often political decisions and teething problems plague a planned smooth introduction into service. The German Luftwaffe has found this to be the case with its A400M transport aircraft and faced some tough technical challenges.

Additionally, German media has, over the years, painted a dark picture of

it faster than the C-160D predecessor with a greater range, extended further with aerial refuelling capability.

However, varying specifications per country and political differences slowed down the process and Lockheed left the programme in 1989, focusing on further upgrading its C-130. Soon afterwards, Alenia from Italy and Casa from Spain joined the group, but eventually Italy also quit the programme. The Italian government went on to procure the C-130J Hercules. On May 27, 2003, an order was finally given to produce a total of 180 aircraft. First flight was scheduled for February 2008 followed by delivery of the first aircraft, to France, in October 2009. Production of the aircraft was to be centred in Seville, Spain.

Powerful Motors

During the A400's development phase, an increasing emphasis on the aircraft's tactical role led to the decision to use turboprop engines instead of the initially planned jets or turbofans. However, one of the first challenges for the manufacturers was the lack of turboprops capable of propelling an A400 aircraft at a cruise speed of Mach 0.78 spun by the very powerful Europrop International TP400-D6 engine rated at 11,000shp. First choice was the SNECMA M138, but this modified M88 engine could not meet the A400M's weight or specific fuel consumption targets. Consequently, Airbus Military issued a new request for proposal (RFP) in April 2002. Even though Pratt & Whitney Canada responded with its proven PW180, the completely new TP400-D6 was selected.

Design of the TP400-D6 is revolutionary. The majority of propeller driven aircraft have all their propellers turning in the same direction. Not so on the A400M. The two propellers on each wing of the A400M counter rotate, a functionality achieved using a Propeller Gear Box (PGB) fitted to two of the engines which turn the propeller on that engine in the opposite direction. All four engines are identical and turn in the same direction, eliminating the need to have two different-handed engines, simplifying maintenance and supply costs.

To help the A400M's certification to civil standards, Airbus decided to reduce the programme's risk by flight-testing the TP400-D6 on a flying test bed contracted to Marshall Aerospace and Defense Group. Airbus Military

specified 700 parameters to be tested and Marshall added another 200. Many factors led to the first flight test of the new TP400-D6 engine on a highly modified C-130K Hercules slipping by 22 months. A design error meant that the engine used for the test did not correspond to the specifications for production-series engines and there were problems with the engine controls.

Eventually, on December 17, 2008, the specially converted C-130K Hercules, RAF serial number XV208, took to the sky on the first of 18 test flights.

Final assembly of the first A400M began at the Seville plant in early 2007 and a roll out ceremony, attended by the late King Juan Carlos of Spain took place on June 26, 2008.

Dogged by Delays

The programme continued to be dogged by delays, schedule adjustments and financial pressures. For example, the production of the fuselage had to be stopped for design changes to be made. Because of measures implemented to compensate for serious vibration caused by the powerful TP400-D6 engines, the fuselage weight increased and became too heavy.

On January 9, 2009, Airbus Military announced that the projected date for the first delivery had been postponed from 2009 to at least 2012. Finally, in January 2011, serial production formally commenced and the first A400M for the Armée de l'Air was officially handed over on September 30, 2013.

Tragedy struck the programme on May 9, 2015 when the 23rd production A400M aircraft, the third for Turkey, crashed on take-off for a pre-delivery test flight from Seville airport, killing four crew members and seriously injuring two more. The pilots had reported a technical fault and asked ATC for permission to land, but the aircraft hit an electricity pylon while attempting an emergency landing. Several reports suggested that as many as three of the aircraft's four engines failed during the A400M's departure. Analysis of the flight data recorders proved that incorrectly installed engine control software caused the fatal crash. Investigators confirmed that engines one, two and three experienced a power freeze after take-off and did not respond to the crew's attempts to control the power setting in the normal way. The key scenario

the new workhorse with epithets such as 'expensive non-seller', 'loser' and 'headache file'. But was this negative press justified? Increasingly the answer is no. Problems have and are being solved and an increasing number of aircraft and aircrew are available for service.

A400: A Piece of History

The original plans for a new multinational-developed transport aircraft date back to 1982 when Aérospatiale, British Aerospace, Lockheed and Messerschmitt-Bölkow-Blohm started making plans for a new transport aircraft to replace the C-130 Hercules and Transall C-160. The new aircraft would be positioned between the C-130 Hercules and C-17 Globemaster. One of the taglines for the A400M was that it could transport what the C-130 could not and to places the C-17 could not land. In fact, an A400M can carry more cargo and move

ABOVE • *The Luftwaffe's first A400M serial number 54+01 (msn 018) after its roll-out from the Airbus production line at San Pablo-Sevilla airport north in late 2014.*
AIRBUS

examined by investigators was that the torque calibration parameter data was accidentally wiped on three engines when the engine software was being installed at Airbus's facilities, preventing the full authority digital engine control from operating. A400Ms in service with air forces across the world were grounded during the crash investigation but Airbus decided to show the world that the aircraft was safe and resumed flying two days after the crash with its own test aircraft.

Luftwaffe Service

In January 2011, the German parliament reduced its A400M requirement to 40 aircraft. Under its contract to buy the A400, Germany is obliged to accept all 53 machines it signed for and tried to sell the surplus aircraft to other nations, one of which was South Africa, but a deal fell through.

German support structure was planned for 40 machines. Storing the 13 surplus aircraft would cost money. As a result, the German Federal Ministry of Defense (BMVg) evaluated an alternative plan, a multinational transport wing loosely based on the European Air Transport Command based at Eindhoven Air Base in the Netherlands where seven countries, including Germany, work together.

The plan involved pooling the 13-surplus aircraft at Lechfeld Air Base. There was however no firm plan and the BMVg calculated the cost of operating these aircraft.

An initial estimate put the price tag at €505m for configuration adaption, maintenance, staff, and €150m for infrastructure changes at a future air base.

A fleet of 40 aircraft requires just one base. Located in central Germany, Wunstorf was chosen to be upgraded to house the nation's A400s.

The Luftwaffe gave-up on the plan and the remaining 13 A400 aircraft are expected to be delivered to the Luftwaffe's Air Transport Wing 62 (ATW 62) by 2026.

Components of ATW 62 include a Flying Group consisting of four flying squadrons, a Technical Group with two technical squadrons for line and base maintenance, a Supply and Transport Squadron and a Training Company which operates a Full Flight Simulator for pilot training, and a Cargo Hold Trainer-Enhanced for the training of the technical loadmasters and the ground crews.

According to a ministry report to parliament, the European A400M programme is years behind schedule, with Germany's share of the costs having risen from an initial estimate

of €8.1bn to €9.6bn. The report also stated that each aircraft was estimated to cost €181m, up from an initial €153m.

At the time, Reuters reported that Tobias Lindner, a member of the Green party and the budget committee claimed: "The renegotiation of the A400M contract in 2010 had been based on false expectations about the airplane's export prospects. The A400M is and remains a problem child."

The first A400M in German service was delivered to Wunstorf on December 19, 2014 and the second arrived a year later.

According to the original delivery plan Germany should have received 11 A400Ms in 2016 and a total of 17 by the end of 2017. However, by the summer of 2017 only ten had been delivered to Wunstorf, all of which were allocated to the European Air Transport Command based at Eindhoven Air Base in the Netherlands.

The first two aircraft were temporarily grounded after inspections found heavy engine wear in the PGB after only 365 and 189 hours of operations respectively. An interim fix was certified in July 2016.

The European Aviation Safety Agency (EASA) now requires initial inspections of the aeroplanes after 650 flight hours, up from 100 hours, with follow-up inspections to be required every 150 hours, up from the 20-hour cycle imposed after the PGB issue emerged.

Airbus, together with the Italian gearbox producer Avio Aero (owned by General Electric), has been working on a permanent solution.

An improved gearbox was fitted to the ninth Luftwaffe machine and all subsequent aircraft. The first eight Luftwaffe A400M aircraft were retrofitted with the improved PGB.

The first Luftwaffe A400 pilots were trained by Airbus in Seville, followed by another tranche at Wunstorf. Today, Luftwaffe A400 pilots undertake their tactical training at Base Aérienne 123 Orléans in France and logistics training at Wunstorf.

Currency on the type is maintained with a minimum of 70 flying hours per year, and on average the pilots log double that. ATW 62 is funded for 185 pilots and 120 loadmasters.

Capability Road Map

BELOW • *Above • An A400M test aircraft dispenses a salvo of flares during a photo shoot to show the system's flare dispersal around the aircraft.* AIRBUS

The sixth Luftwaffe A400M, delivered in December 2016, was the first certified for tactical operations and able to fly in areas subject to military threats. All the earlier aircraft are being updated to the new standard.

Of the 53 aircraft ordered, 24 are expected to be fitted with a defensive-aids sub-system (DASS) incorporating a missile warning system, radar warning receiver, and an expendables-dispensing system to eject flares and radar-confusing chaff.

In July 2019, Germany was the first nation to successfully qualify the A400M as an aerial refuelling aircraft for use abroad after a 14-day test programme. At the beginning of September that year, the A400 replaced the A310 in the Operation Inherent Resolve tanker mission, a tasking the A400 held until March 31, 2020.

In November 2019, after completion of Luftwaffe operational testing, the BAAINBw approved another capability package that included landing on unpaved runways, extending night-vision to desert areas, depositing loads using gravity methods, a tactical data link and an infrared protection equipment.

The following month, a Luftwaffe A400M equipped with the electronic infrared protection system designed to counter surface-to-air missiles, landed at Al-Asrak Air Base, Jordan for the first time for tasking in support of Operation Inherent Resolve.

In mid-2020, the A400 partner nations approved the A400M's New Standard Operating Clearance 2.0 certification standard, its first major capability update since service introduction in October 2013.

On September 8, 2021, the A400M's New Standard Operating Clearance 2.5 (NSOC 2.5) was approved by OCCAR-EA. This so-called type-acceptance declares to Airbus that the contractually agreed requirements for this aircraft standard have been met.

NSOC 2.5 provides the ability to simultaneously drop 116 paratroopers from the side doors in a single pass with automatically deployed parachutes; the ability to drop loads using the pull-out method; fly independent instrument approaches in instrument meteorological condition; further optimisation of the self-protection system; and approval of an initial qualification for automatic low-level flight.

Some of these capabilities were subsequently released to service by the Federal Office of Bundeswehr Equipment, Information Technology and In-Service Support or BAAINBw.

New A400M aircraft delivered from 2023 should be configured with NSOC 3.0 and all other Luftwaffe A400Ms will be fully upgraded to this standard.

Since mid-2022, Air Transport Wing 62 has undertaken tactical and strategic patient air transport with one aircraft held on standby around the clock to provide medical evacuation to wounded or injured soldiers from the Bundeswehr's areas of operation.

On November 16, 2022, the Bundeswehr took delivery of its 40th A400M following full acceptance seven days earlier, a time when Airbus was completing the A400M's aerial delivery capabilities, such as automatic combat unloading and high-altitude airdrops of cargo and parachutists.

A400 Capabilities Include

- Self-defence system improvement.
- Capability to airdrop cargo loads and paratroopers.
- Ability to operate on unprepared runways.
- Fly as low as 150 feet.
- Aerial-refuel other aircraft with hose-and-drogue systems housed in pods mounted on the wingtips and centrally mounted.
- Safely take-off and land in extremely high temperatures.
- Flight plan preparation by a separate team at Wunstorf using a system with the ability to upload the flight plan anywhere in the world and subsequently carry out the mission.

Elefantes

Mark Ayton provides an overview of the C295-equipped Esquadron 502, a busy multirole squadron at the heart of the Força Aerea Portuguesa.

Standing amidst five C295 aircraft undergoing maintenance in Esquadron 502's hangar, one could be excused for thinking the unit is a transport squadron. After all, the C295, built by Airbus at Sevilla-San Pablo, is a twin-turboprop tactical transport aircraft. However, five of the Montijo-based squadron's 12 aircraft are configured to use a roll-on, roll-off mission system, which when fitted enables the aeroplane to conduct maritime surveillance. Looking around the main hangar, one aircraft was configured with two radomes, one mounted on the nose and a second under the forward fuselage. Esquadron 502 was formed in 1955 and uses Elefantes (Elephants) for its nickname.

Elephant Missions

Discussing the various roles undertaken by the C295, Major Marco Carvalho, then the squadron's commanding officer, said the aircraft provides national support in transport, medical evacuation (medevac), search and rescue (SAR) and maritime surveillance missions. Medevac and SAR tasking involves one dedicated aircraft held on 30-minute readiness in daytime and 120 minutes at night.

Maritime surveillance sorties are flown on average four or five times per week at varying times of the day over the Atlantic Ocean to the west and southwest of Portugal. Patrols are rarely conducted to find anything specific but are planned randomly. Explaining the process, Maj Carvalho said: "If, for example, we detect pollution on the surface with the SLAR [Sideward Looking Radar] we can see the extent and coordinate with the navy to send a ship to the location to deal with the pollution.

"If we see illegal activity, we remain on scene to capture information while coordinating with the relevant authorities and providing them with the information. We patrol the area out to 10W [Latitude 10o west] and can check ships and fishing boats and how they are working from Africa and the Mediterranean Sea in a five to six-hour window."

Esquadron 502 also flies at least one weekly mission to provide Portuguese Army paratroopers with low-altitude and high-altitude paradrop training.

Island Support

Portugal has two autonomous regions comprising two archipelagos located in the North Atlantic: Madeira (970km/600 miles to the west) and the Azores (1,450km/900 miles to the southwest). The Força Aerea Portuguesa operates from Aerodromo Manobra 3 Porto Santo (Madeira) and Base Aerea 4 Lajes (Azores) and retains an EH101 Merlin at each and two C295s at Lajes. Esquadron 502 airlifts cargo and 20 to 30 personnel to Porto Santo and Lajes on average every 15 days.

The Lajes-based detachment is kept busy with medical evacuation and SAR missions. Medical evacuation sorties are common, because Horta is the only island in the Azores archipelago with a hospital. Many medevac sorties are flown in response to people who have fallen sick or suffered injury on ships underway in the Atlantic Ocean. First response is usually provided

BELOW • *One of Esquadron 502's C295s, serial number 16702.* AIRBUS

by Esquadron 751, the Força Aerea Portuguesa's heavy helicopter squadron, which has an EH101 Merlin based at Porto Santo and Lajes. If a patient requires specialist medical treatment only available on the mainland, Esquadron 502 flies him or her to Lisbon.

SAR missions mounted in response to distress calls from boats, yachts, and ships in the Atlantic involve a C295 and a Merlin helicopter, as explained by Maj Carvalho: "The C295 takes-off first to find the boat and remains on scene in communication with the boat. Part of the aircrew's task at this stage is to ensure the sick person or people requiring rescue are prepared and ready to be lifted from the deck, and that the boat is turned around in the direction required so the helicopter can hover upwind of the boat for stability. The helicopter is at greater risk when it's slowly manoeuvring close to the boat with a rescue swimmer on the cable. If an accident happens and the helicopter ditches, we are ready to immediately launch life rafts to help the helicopter crew.

"It's a complex and expensive mission, because in order for the helicopter to fly up to 350 nautical miles and return, both the C295 and the Merlin are airborne for six hours."

Operating restrictions apply to both the Merlin and the C295. At the airfield of departure, wind strength over 40kts makes landing the C295 challenging. There are only two airfields in the Azores to choose from. According to Maj Carvalho, if the pilot is facing a 40kts cross wind it's always challenging to land: "Sometimes we shut the engines down immediately after leaving the runway, because we cannot safely taxi to parking, but there are not many missions like that."

Maj Carvalho said ceiling and visibility restrictions limit the aircraft at the scene: "We can work down to 500ft [150m] above the sea level, because the helicopter works at 100 to 200ft [30 to 60m] above the boat; but wind conditions down at 500ft are not a factor, because we are in an orbit."

Africa

On January 5, 2015, Esquadron 502 started at two-month deployment to Bamako, the capital of Mali to support United Nations' operations in the African country. The C295 deployment followed a five-month stint by C-130H-equipped Esquadron 501.

Esquadron 502 was deployed throughout January and February 2015 undertaking typical transport work in support of peacekeeping operations. The entire deployment comprised two detachments each with two crews and one aircraft. The detachment was tasked to provide medical evacuation 24 hours per day, seven days a week, enabled by its night-vision capability.

The C295 held-up well to the rigours of flying from dusty landing strips around Mali with no serious maintenance problems encountered during the two-month operation. To counter serviceability issues encountered during flight operations, some of the aircrews are also trained to perform certain maintenance procedures such as changing a flat tyre. If a problem developed with one of the aircraft's systems, they could troubleshoot the fault, pass details to the maintenance officer at Bamako and arrange to bring spares on another aircraft with other maintainers to help.

When flying into Kidal and Tessalit, ground safety procedures were always in place and armed field protection troops were carried on board the C295. All loading and offloading was conducted with both engines running. Such operations were done more aggressively than usual to minimise the risk of attack, dust ingestion and overheating; temperatures on some days were 47°C.

During operations at austere locations the aircraft is at most risk during landing and take-off from rockets and MANPADs. To ✈

16702

counter such threats, aircrews flew different tactics and used infrared countermeasures to help defeat any shots fired. The C295 defensive suite includes a radar warning receiver and missile approach warning system.

However, Mali was not the first international operation in which Esquadron 502 participated. In 2010, the European Union (EU) agency dubbed FRONTEX (official title the European Agency for the Management of Operational Cooperation at the External Borders of the Member States of the European

Union) invited Portugal to join its operations. This resulted in the Força Aerea Portuguesa flying maritime surveillance missions throughout the Mediterranean between May and November 2011 looking for migrant people trying to reach the EU from North Africa and Syria. According to the EU, the agency promotes, coordinates, and develops European border management in line with the EU fundamental rights charter applying the concept of integrated border management by helping

border authorities from different EU countries work together.

Operating from Malaga, Spain, the Italian island of Sicily, and Greece, Esquadron 502 conducted patrols lasting up to five hours to spot boats underway in the Mediterranean and assess what each boat was carrying.

Maj Carvalho recalled how the crews could see the people onboard the boats and expressed the satisfaction felt by the crews who felt they were helping the people: "We carry medical provisions and life rafts and dropped them in the SAR role while waiting on scene to direct naval ships to the position to pick them up. That happened many times."

Training

Esquadron 502 is a busy squadron with ongoing national tasking and detachments to Lajes. Consequently, much of its proficiency training must be conducted during other tasking. Pilots follow a six-monthly flight proficiency programme covering all the unit's mission profiles like SAR, paradropping, special transport and maritime surveillance. Loadmasters, tactical coordinators, and pilots all receive a six-monthly check for each mission profile.

"We try to do most training, 80%, on the job because the crew cover so many aspects in normal missions and can be checked by an instructor on board. The other 20% are tactical missions like cargo drops and employing the aircraft's sensors for tactical scenarios and should be certified on training missions," said Maj Carvalho.

Maj Carvalho said the Mali deployment was important for training crews to counter the threat level: "When you operate in a place with a threat level everything is different. It was important for Portugal to deploy the C295 to Mali to show the aircraft can be used in various scenarios; fly into places to collect people or insert special forces at night using NVGs. So, it's flexible.

"I also want to highlight the search and rescue missions we do with the Merlins, because they are really, really challenging and happen once or twice a month and save lives. Coordination between the helicopter and the C295 to provide safety to the Merlin, so it can remain on scene for as long as possible in the area to pick people from a boat and return home, is important. Everyone is committed to that," he said.

LEFT • *Each six-bladed Hamilton Standard 586-F propeller is driven by a Pratt & Whitney Canada PW127G turboprop rated at 2,645hp (1,972kW).* AIRBUS

C295 Characteristics

Length	24.50m (80ft 3in)
Wingspan	25.81m (84ft 8in)
Height	8.60m (28ft 3in)
Wing area	59m² (634.8ft²)
Max take-off weight	23,200kg (51,146lb)
Max speed	311kts (576km/h)
Cruise speed	260kts (480km/h)
Payload	4,000kg (8,820lb)
Capacity	71 troops
Range with 3,000kg (6,600lb) payload	2,500nm (4,600km)
Range with 6,000kg (13,200lb) payload	2,000nm (3,700km)
Range with max 9,250kg (20,400lb) payload	700nm (1,300km)
Ferry range	2,900nm (5,400km)
Service ceiling	30,000ft (9,100m)
Take-off run	2,200ft (670m)
Landing run	1,050ft (320m)
Powerplant	Two Pratt & Whitney Canada PW127G turboprops each rated at 2,645hp (1,972kW) driving six-bladed Hamilton Standard 586-F propellers
Crew	Two

Source: Airbus

RIGHT • *The C295 has a fuselage length of 80ft 3in (24.50m) and a wingspan of 84ft 8in (25.81m).* AIRBUS

Mission System and Sensors

When configured for the maritime surveillance role, a Força Aerea Portuguesa C295 is fitted with a modular roll-on, roll-off variant of the fully integrated tactical system called Vigilance Maritime, dubbed VIMAR. This is a mission system applicable to various subsets of surveillance: SAR, maritime patrol, border protection, drug interdiction, immigration control, maritime pollution prevention and the protection of fisheries and economic zones.

The VIMAR system allows tactical operators to control the aircraft's sensors and provides them with real-time tactical and navigation information by interfacing the aircraft's navigation and communication systems using a data management system. According to Airbus, the system also manages aircraft navigation through the creation of a search pattern, guiding the aircraft to emergency locator signals.

The information is also shown on one of the four LCD displays in the cockpit. The typical setup for a Força Aerea Portuguesa C295 is two consoles.

The C295's satellite communication suite allows data, images and video gathered by a Wescam MX-15 sensor to be sent to a ship or ground station ashore.

Esquadron 502's aircraft configured for maritime surveillance are equipped with three primary sensors: the Elta ELM-2022A radar; Terma SLAR 9000 side-looking airborne radar; and a Wescam MX-15 EO/IR system.

The ELM-2022A is an all-weather, day and night X-band multimode airborne radar system optimised for long-range maritime surveillance and detection of large targets up to 200nm (370km) away, but equally capable of detecting a small target in adverse sea conditions. Elta says the ELM-2022A is capable of automatically tracking all detected targets and penetrating clouds, rain, smoke, smog, fog, and manmade camouflage.

In addition to maritime surveillance, the ELM-2022A supports, maritime law enforcement, fishery and economic zone patrolling, SAR, air-to-ground and air-to-air surveillance missions.

Modes of operation are range profiling; inverse synthetic aperture radar, which provides automatic vessel classification at the radar's range in day and night conditions; strip and spot synthetic aperture radar imaging and ground moving target indicator used to provide intelligence, surveillance, and reconnaissance support for ground operations; navigation and weather.

The SLAR 9000 is a side-looking sensor capable of searching 25nm (45km) to the side of the aircraft, which covers a huge area in a short time. All SLAR data is shown in real time with the image in one of two modes: waterfall, in which the aircraft is in the top of the image; or a synthetic map with north up. The tactical operator can zoom, pan, and scroll the image, which is fully annotated with data fed by the aircraft's other sensors.

The chin-mounted Wescam MX-15 EO/IR sensor is the primary system used by the tactical operator to detect, classify, identify, and track targets day or night.

The MX-15 turret is gyro-stabilised and provides an unrestricted 360° azimuth field of view for all four of its integrated sensors: infrared; continuous zoom TV colour camera; spotter scope monochrome TV camera; and automatic identification system.

In auto-scan mode the turret automatically sweeps the ocean or land surface, at an angle and rate set by the tactical operator. When a target is detected, the MX-15 automatically locks on and starts to auto-track.

Franco-Italian Turboprops

An overview of turboprop aircraft built by ATR, the world's number one regional aircraft manufacturer.

ATR was formed as a joint venture and equal partnership between Aeritalia and Aerospatiale, which had each been working on regional airliner projects – the AIT 230 and AS 35, respectively. The Italian and French firms, now part of Leonardo and Airbus, respectively, originally established ATR (Aerei da Trasporto Regionale or Avions de Transport Régional) in October-November 1981 as a groupement d'intérêt économique under French law, with the aim of developing a family of regional airliners.

Not only had the two companies been developing their own aircraft, but they were aware that De Havilland Canada, British Aerospace, Saab, Embraer, Dornier, and Fokker were also vying for orders for their own 29-78 seaters.

ATR 42

The first aircraft to be produced by the new partnership was the ATR 42, which had its maiden flight on August 16, 1984, from Toulouse-Francazal airport. Certification was granted by Italian and French authorities in September 1985, and the type entered service with Air Littoral – based in Le Castellet, France – on December 9, 1985. The type can carry between 42 and 50 passengers, depending on the internal fit.

Production airframes were termed the ATR 42-300, having a greater payload range and a higher take-off weight than the prototypes, while the ATR 42-320 differs in having the more powerful Pratt & Whitney Canada PW121 engines (as opposed to the standard PW120), for better hot and high performance. Other versions have included the ATR 42QC, which is a quick-change freight/

passenger version of the ATR 42-300 and the ATR 42 Freighter, which is a fully modified airframe for cargo use only.

ATR 72

The ATR 72 is a larger version of the original ATR 42 aircraft, produced to increase the seating capacity from 48 to 78 by stretching the fuselage by 15ft, increasing the wingspan, adding more powerful Pratt & Whitney Canada PW124 engines, and increasing fuel capacity by about 10%. Its design was announced in 1986, and the prototype – a converted ATR 42 – made its maiden flight on October 27, 1988, from Toulouse-Francazal airport. Exactly one year later, the type entered service with Finnish airline Karair, which was taken over by Finnair in 1996. Despite the ATR 42 having a two-year head start,

BELOW • *An ATR 72-500 in a livery denoting 40 years of making a difference at Toulouse-Francazal airport.* ATR/PIERRE BATHÉ

ABOVE • *An ATR 42-600 belonging to Fort Lauderdale-Hollywood-based Silver Airways at Toulouse-Francazal.*
ATR/PIERRE BATHÉ

RIGHT • *ATR 72-600F EI-GUL (msn 1653) is operated by Ireland-based ASL Airlines as a Fedex Feeder.*
ATR/PIERRE BATHÉ

the larger ATR 72 has proved a bigger sales success for the Franco-Italians, accounting for more than two-thirds of the 1,600+ turboprops produced since 1984.

500 Series

As more modern materials, interiors, electronics, and avionics became available, ATR decided to make improvements to its turboprops in the shape of the -500 series. The ATR 42-500 was the first significantly improved version of the aircraft and featured a revised interior, more powerful Pratt & Whitney Canada PW127Es (for a substantially increased

cruising speed) driving six-bladed propellers, a 1,000nm maximum range, the Electronic Flight Information System (EFIS) cockpit, elevators, and rudders of the stretched ATR 72 (described separately), plus new brakes and landing gear and strengthened wing and fuselage for greater weights.

The first ATR 42-500 delivery was in October 1995, with the ATR 72-500 following two years later. The interior was completely redesigned, to create 40% more overhead baggage space and a more spacious feel to the cabin. The use of new materials and tuned vibration dampers resulted in a reduction in cabin noise and vibration

– aided by the new propellers. The ATR 42-500 has a standard layout that accommodates 48 passengers with a 30in pitch, while the ATR 72-500 seats 68 with a 31in pitch. Both have a 90% commonality of spares, while pilots have a common type rating between the two -500 versions. This enables airlines to operate a mix of aircraft with limited additional costs.

One of the lessons learnt from earlier models resulted in the engine manufacturer, Pratt & Whitney Canada, fitting a propeller brake, which enables the starboard propeller to be locked on the ground whilst the engine is still running – and therefore provide any internal power necessary. This facility – known as 'hotel mode' – has several benefits, among them obviating the need for an auxiliary power unit (APU), thus saving weight, space (and cost), plus centre of gravity considerations in placing the APU.

Aircraft Assembly

Major sub-assemblies of the aircraft are manufactured in France and Italy, and joined in Toulouse, from where their maiden flights are made.

Leonardo's manufacturing facilities in Pomigliano d'Arco, near Naples, Italy, produce the fuselage and tail sections, and the wings are assembled by Stelia Aerospace in Bordeaux. Other assemblies are fitted to the major

LEFT • *Prototype ATR 72-600 msn 1157 on take-off from Toulouse-Francazal airport.*
ATR/MÉLODY CHUNLAUD

parts while on the production line at Toulouse. The engines come from Pratt & Whitney Canada and the propellers arrive from Hamilton Standard in Connecticut.

Aircraft generally leave the factory fitted out internally, with Sicma supplying the seats but customers can specify alternative manufacturers if required. For instance, aircraft destined for the United States usually have their seats fitted in North America.

From arrival at Toulouse, it takes between three and four months to complete the assembly process, ready for delivery of the finished article.

600 Series

The company received EASA type certification for the ATR 72-600 in 2011, with the ATR 42 following in mid-2012. Deliveries of the first ATR 72-600s began in August 2011, with Royal Air Maroc accepting the first production example, while deliveries of ATR 42-600s started in November 2012, with the first of two aircraft for Tanzania's Precision Air.

All -600 aircraft are equipped with the Armonia cabin, which was specially developed for the manufacturer by Italian designer Giugiaro. It features wider and lighter seats, larger overhead bins, and an optional dual class interior. The flight deck features five wide LCD screens replacing the -500 series' electronic flight instrument system. The aircraft is powered by the uprated Pratt & Whitney Canada PW127M engine, which has since been offered as an option on the -500, while also becoming the standard fit on the -600. It has been designed to deliver improved performance, particularly on short runways, and incorporates a boost function that provides a 5% increase in power when operating in hot and high conditions.

Other Options

ATR has long offered freighters – first doing so at Farnborough in 2002. However, the Franco-Italian framer only converted its passenger products to cargo carriers prior to December 2020. It has since dispatched freighters to FedEx, one to ASL Airlines Ireland and two stateside to Empire Airlines. The US giant ordered 30 of the custom couriers.

With the Pan-European plane producer pointing out that almost two-fifths of its customers operate in remote areas and islands, it announced a short take-off and landing (STOL) variant at the 2019 Paris Air Show. The ATR 42-600S reduces the minimum runway length required from 3,445ft to 2,625ft,

BELOW • *ATR is developing a next generation family of aircraft dubbed EVO.*
ATR/EVO

RIGHT • *The Hokkaido Air Company (HAC) operates three ATR 42-600s which are painted with Japan Airline and oneworld markings.* ATR/MÉLODY CHUNLAUD

thanks to a redesigned tail unit and enhanced brakes. The enthusiasm for the niche version resulted in 17 orders during the show, quickly climbing to 20. Launch customer Air Tahiti was originally expecting to take delivery of its first ATR 42-600S in 2022 but it is now likely to happen in late 2024.

Speaking about the STOL variant soon after its launch, Zuzana Hrnkova, vice-president of marketing at ATR said: "The ATR 42-600 needs something like 3,675ft for take-off and landing... We studied other turboprops with 30-50 seats – which included the Saab 340 and Saab 2000, the Dash 8/Q100/Q200/ Q300 and so on – and all those aircraft

are flown in short take-off and landing conditions. We discussed with carriers who fly in these conditions, and they told us that on some routes with a 30-seater, they do so from 2,625ft runways. Thus, our first design target was to embody an improvement to the ATR 42-600 to make it take-off and land on a runway of this size, with a payload equivalent to current operations. The next task was to enable it to take-off and land on a 2,953ft runway with a full payload of 48 passengers.

"We then looked at what we needed to modify on the aeroplane to make this happen, to fulfil those

two main criteria. The first thing was to increase engine power, so we have the same rating on the ATR 42-600S as on the ATR 72-600, which is 2,750shp – an increase of 350shp over the current aeroplane.

"When you have more engine thrust, you need to improve the lateral controllability during take-off and landing. For this, we must increase rudder efficiency, so there are modifications to do here, to improve control. Next is a further reduction of the take-off distance. We do this through using the Flap 25 position, to increase lift and therefore reduce distance. For landing, we worked ✈

on the spoilers and, of course, the brakes, so we have implemented automatic braking, to improve the stopping distance. Those are the major modifications for the ATR 42-600S."

Coming up with this model has, of course, been a reaction to demand. Hrnkova outlined the key markets for the aircraft. "We currently have two types of market. One is Northern Europe (the Scandinavian countries) and Canada as well – the areas with cold conditions during the wintertime. Then there are the Pacific Island countries. ATR has had some success before in the latter region and believes this new capability will add to that. In the Pacific islands, the carriers also fly 19-seaters, such as the De Havilland Canada DHC-6 Twin Otter, which are not pressurised, and they have shown an interest in the ATR 42-600S. So, it's not just a replacement for 30-50 seaters on short take-off and landing [runways], which was our initial focus. When we started to talk with the airlines, they told us that

they are interested in replacing small aeroplanes to rationalise their fleets and use our aircraft not only for STOL flights, but to access their entire networks."

ClearVision

Fog has always posed a major obstacle for aviation in the Channel Islands, and Guernsey's airline Aurigny is familiar with the cancellations, delays, and diversions it can cause. In this respect, the airline purchased three ATR 72-600 turboprops, the first examples of the aircraft equipped with ATR's ClearVision enhanced vision system (EVS).

ATR's ClearVision is designed to provide pilots with improved situational awareness in poor visibility. It uses a fuselage-mounted camera to display an augmented external view in real-time to a head-mounted visor, Skylens, worn by the pilot.

Announced in 2015, ClearVision is supplied by Elbit Systems and is a line-fit option on both the ATR 72-600 and its smaller ATR 42-600 sister

aircraft, the two variants that make up the latest ATR 600 Series family. The manufacturer also offers ClearVision as a retrofit for ATR 600 Series aircraft already in service.

The Skylens wearable display presents high-resolution information, images and video on a high transparency visor that replaces the traditional head-up display.

Aircraft equipped with ClearVision can take-off and land in low-visibility conditions and in locations non EVS-equipped aircraft previously could not approach. Hrnkova told the author: "The system offers pilots improved situational awareness and reduces operating minima so [it] increases airport accessibility without requiring expensive upgrades to an airport's infrastructure."

In addition to the EVS, ClearVision also offers a synthetic vision system (SVS) that provides the pilot's head-up display with digital images of terrain and obstacles from an extensive database; operators can also opt for a Combined Vision System (CVS) that blends both the EVS and SVS.

Aurigny's ATRs are equipped only with the EVS element of ClearVision, and not the SVS nor the full CVS, but there is an obvious benefit of the EVS for the carrier and other airlines whose operations are regularly affected by fog.

An Aurigny spokesperson told the author: "Whilst not fundamental to our purchase decision, given that Guernsey is often affected by fog the ClearVision technology obviously adds more value to the new aircraft."

Aurigny saw the potential of ClearVision at first hand when ATR conducted a trial in Guernsey with one of its ATR 72-600 test aircraft equipped

ABOVE • Guernsey-based Aurigny Air Services operates three ATR 72-600s including G-OATR (msn 1580). ATR/PIERRE

LEFT • Greater economy and sustainability are two objectives for the ATR EVO family of aircraft. ATR/EVO

RIGHT • *ATR 72-600F in FedEx colours over the Pyrenees during a functional check flight from Toulouse.* ATR/PIERRE BATHÉ

with the system, the aircraft landing on the island in reduced visibility. According to ATR, the trial showed ClearVision could reduce the number of cancelled landings in Guernsey by 50%.

At the time, Aurigny said: "The ClearVision system will have to go through a certification phase. In time, we expect it to help save us money in reducing delays and disruption to our customers in inclement weather. Once the system is certified for commercial operational use and our pilots have completed the necessary training it will reduce service disruption during periods of reduced visibility. The minima will reduce to 1,148ft [350m] runway visual range and 100ft [30m] decision height."

Aurigny was the launch customer for ClearVision and received its first ATR 72-600 equipped with the technology in October 2019.

Hrnkova told the author only one other operator has ordered ClearVision so far, but said the company is 'confident' more customers will follow, saying: "ATRs are already the best aircraft at serving airports that are either isolated or surrounded by challenging terrain. This new technology will bring more advantages to operators accessing these remote locations, improving links to local economies and the lives of the communities these airlines serve."

Avionics Upgrades

ClearVision is not the only innovation ATR has put into its products recently. Hrnkova noted ATRs are delivered as standard with the company's Standard 3 Avionics Suite, which offers required navigation performance with authorisation required (RNP-AR) 0.3. This enables pilots to follow trajectories to within an accuracy of 0.2nm (0.4km) and permits reduced minimums compared to conventional approaches.

The Standard 3 Avionics also features automatic dependent surveillance-broadcast out compatibility, a traffic collision and avoidance system and localiser performance with vertical guidance. The latter system lets crews carry out precision approaches with minimums of up to 200ft (60m) visibility based on GPS information, enabling an aircraft to be guided on vertical and horizontal axes without the need for support from a ground station.

There is a satellite-based augmentation system and a vertical navigation functionality coupled to the autopilot, which provides vertical guidance managed by the aircraft's navigation calculator in the flight management system to better define descent and approach trajectories.

Automatic checklists, automated monitoring of terrain, traffic and weather, automated failure detection and automated pop-ups on the display are further standard features.

Options include aircraft communications addressing and reporting, Class 2 electronic flight bag compatibility and an airport navigation function showing the aircraft's position on an airport map.

Cabin

Innovations continue in the cabin. In 2018, ATR certified and introduced new seats called Neo-Classic and Neo-Prestige as standard on all new ATRs. These offer 18in (457mm) intra-armrest width and they are, Hrnkova says, "a first for a turboprop, reaching the standard of single-aisle aircraft if not even exceeding [it] compared to some airframes".

The Aurigny spokesperson said the Guernsey airline's aircraft will have 72 seats and be configured in 18 rows of four. The seat pitch will be a combination of 29in (736mm) and 30in (762mm), adding: "The design of the new seats means they have thinner seat backs, thus creating slightly extra legroom. The smart cabin design also benefits from extra capacity in the overhead lockers."

Another new onboard feature is the Cabinstream in-flight entertainment (IFE) system, for which Afrijet is launch customer. Cabinstream provides IFE content wirelessly from a server installed in the overhead baggage hold. Hrnkova noted it doesn't provide full internet connectivity, but passengers can connect their device to download or stream content from the server such as TV series in HD,

music, newspapers, and travel guides. The Cabinstream box weighs less than 6kg (13lb), has 12-hour battery life and is designed to be easy to install and remove.

Systems innovations

Some of the most significant recent changes to the ATR Series 600 involve improvements to the Multi-Function Computer (MFC), the turboprop's electronic architecture, with the introduction of a Next Generation Multi-Function Computer (MFC NG).

The MFC, a feature of the ATR's systems architecture since 1992, provides centralised computing and data communication to host applications that perform aircraft functions. It constantly receives information from aircraft components and systems, interprets it and sends commands around the aircraft while also monitoring their performance.

The MFC NG has a similar hardware configuration to its predecessor but features new software. A multi-core processor provides the requisite performance level as well as scope for embedding independent applications and ethernet connectivity with a new data-loading and maintenance tool.

The initial version of the MFC NG features three applications: one for systems control and monitoring, another for systems maintenance and fault memorisation (including enhanced fault isolation and troubleshooting plus embedded management of the multifunction display units) and a bus power control application.

The MFC NG is designed to provide a more user-friendly maintenance tool tailored to a user, allow for supplementary applications to be added

LEFT • *Head-on shot of an ATR 42-500.*
ATR/PIERRE BATHÉ

in the future and offer a maintenance benefit from being smaller and lighter than the previous MFC.

Embracing Digital

Digitalisation, especially the Internet of Things, mobile devices and applications and augmented reality, is a huge area in aerospace, just as it is many other industries. How is ATR using the digital revolution to improve its products?

Hrnkova said: "All aircraft on the production line can be tracked in real-time with the help of small communicating devices, which removes the hassle of verifying how they have been moved, which happens constantly.

"Digitalisation may also be used to develop new services for our customers. One example is the development of maintenance-oriented activities based on data analytics, to identify system failures and parts in need of replacement before they break down. This will enable maintenance teams to prepare beforehand, thereby significantly reducing aircraft time on the ground and optimising costs."

Hrnkova added that ATR is also looking at finding new ways to use operational data to give customers better insights into their operations. ATR now has a support package called Flight Data Monitoring that enables operators to identify and resolve emerging issues to improve performance and cost efficiency. The system provides operators with detailed recommendations and advice on specific procedural changes that will reduce aircraft downtime and boost the efficiency of each individual aircraft, based on the data generated across the fleet.

Hrnkova said: "Examples of recommendations could include how much fuel is required for a specific flight to avoid carrying excess fuel, or how to optimise an approach phase to ensure it is as smooth as possible. The Flight Data Monitoring package can also optimise maintenance costs, by generating improvements to training and troubleshooting procedures.

"It could also feed into predictive maintenance, enabling operators to avoid failures, improve fleet availability and increase overall equipment lifetime through the prevention of collateral wear."

Continuous Development

Hrnkova said ATR's priority for its product is making its turboprops as

BELOW • *An ATR 72-600 in corporate colours over the French coastline during a photo shoot from Toulouse.*
ATR/ANTHONY PECCHI

ATR Series 600 Characteristics

	ATR 72-600	ATR 42-600
Wingspan	27.05m (88ft 9in)	24.57m (80ft 7in)
Length	27.17m (89ft 2in)	22.67m (74ft 5in)
Height	6m (19ft 8in)	7.59m (24ft 11in)
Max take-off weight (MTOW)	23,000kg (50,705lb)	18,600kg (41,005lb)
Max landing weight	22,350kg (49,273lb)	18,300kg (40,344lb)
Max zero fuel weight	21,000kg (46,296lb)	17,000kg (37,478lb)
Max payload	7,500kg (16,534lb)	5,300kg (11,684lb)
Max fuel load	5,000kg (11,023lb)	4,500kg (9,921lb)
Take-off distance (at MTOW)	3,855ft (1,175m)	3,822ft (1,165m)
Landing distance	3,307ft (1,108m)	3,694ft (1,126m)
Cargo volume	10.6m^3 (374ft^3)	9.6m^3 (339ft^3)
Seating	44-78 seats	30-50 seats
Range	825 nm (1,528km)	716 nm (1,326km)
Cruise speed	275kts	275kts
Ceiling	25,000ft	25,000ft
Engines	Two Pratt & Whitney Canada PW127Ms with Hamilton Sundstrand 568F-1 propellers	Two Pratt & Whitney Canada PW127Ms with Hamilton Sundstrand 568F-1 propellers

Source: ATR

efficient as possible to reduce per-seat operating costs and fulfil operators' expectations. The manufacturer upgraded its ATR 72-600 test aircraft F-WKVK (msn 1157) with the latest new components and avionics systems and equipment. Among the first innovations to be tested on this aircraft was a new air-conditioning management system, designed to reduce aircon maintenance costs by 40%.

Expanding on the digital support described above, introducing new avionics, and upgrading systems are ways to maximise the potential of the current ATR 600 Series variants, but what about further development of the aircraft family itself?

The manufacturer launched a new version of the ATR 42-600 with improved short take-off and landing capabilities designated the ATR 42-600S which made its maiden flight from Toulouse-Francazal Airport on May 11, 2022, lasting 2 hours and 15 minutes.

Hrnkova said: "We are confident that our policy of continuous development will continue to meet the needs of our operators and so we will continue to optimise the existing aircraft."

Future Initiatives

ATR has never been a company that's been seen as creating a revolution – instead, it has provided gradual and modest updates to its two airframes. This aversion to risk taking has, arguably, meant that the turboprop market lags in terms of innovation. However, a considered approach has also secured the company's survival during a time when competitors such as BAE Systems, Bombardier and Saab pulled out of the commercial airliner market, while others such as Fairchild Dornier and Fokker have collapsed.

While ATR holds a monopoly in its sector, what is likely its biggest challenge is yet to come, a reaction to Embraer's clean-sheet turboprop. On May 18, 2022, ATR announced plans to develop the next generation ATR EVO regional aircraft by 2030. The plan foresees a new eco-design that includes a new powerplant with hybrid capability encompassing innovative technologies to enable significant improvements in performance, economics, and sustainability, new propellers and enhanced cabin and systems, it will remain a two-engine turboprop that can be powered by 100% Sustainable Aviation Fuel (SAF).

ATR CEO Stefano Bortoli said: "Our next generation of aircraft will be a step forward in responsible flying through further incremental innovation. When it enters the market, the new ATR EVO will pave the way towards a decarbonised future for aviation.

Key benefits include a 20% overall fuel improvement and 100% SAF compatibility. This means that the aircraft will emit over 50% less CO_2 than a regional jet when powered by kerosene. When using 100% SAF, its emissions will be close to zero."

Fabrice Vautier, ATR senior vice president commercial said: "The ATR EVO will be even more economical, with double digit operating cost savings achieved through 20% lower fuel burn and 20% overall maintenance cost reduction. This means airlines can serve thin routes more profitably, and communities can benefit from more connectivity, more essential services, and more economic development. Our aim is to continue to offer customers and society ever more inclusive and responsible air transportation."

Stéphane Viala, ATR senior vice president engineering added: "We have issued a request for information to the main engine manufacturers for the development of a new powerplant that will combine existing and future generation engine technology. The ATR EVO will feature improved performance in terms of time to climb and an enhanced cabin, with increased use of lighter bio-sourced materials. Recyclability will also be at the heart of our new design.

Guardia di Finanza's New Patroller

Riccardo Niccoli details the Guardia di Finanza's brand new
ATR-Leonardo P-72 patrol aircraft

Italy's customs and economic police, the Guardia di Finanza, uses a small fleet of patrol aircraft to perform an important, but often undervalued role. In the early 1990s, the corps identified the ATR-42MP turboprop as the best suited to meet its operational requirements.

Three ATR-42MP patrol aircraft were acquired, plus another in passenger transport configuration, the first of which was delivered to the Guardia di Finanza in 1995. These aircraft have enabled the service to perform missions to counter illicit maritime trafficking of goods, narcotics, and people, with favourable results. Throughout their service life to date the Guardia di Finanza's ATR-42MP's have operated at high utilisation rates, which more recently has led the corps to determine a new type of more capable aircraft as a replacement.

More ATRs

In 2017, the Corps published an invitation to tender, from which Leonardo emerged as the winner with its ATR-72MP proposal; this was followed in July 2018 by an initial contract for one aircraft, followed on October 9, 2019, by a second contract, worth €150m, for a further three machines.

The first example, ATR-72MP MM.62311 'Grifo 20' was assigned the Italian military designation of P-72B and benefitted from co-financing by the European External Frontiers Fund. The first aircraft was delivered to the Guardia di Finanza on November 27, 2019, followed in early December by the second aircraft MM.62315 'Grifo 21' in green configuration without its missions' systems installed.

With the two aircraft assigned, the Servizio Aereo (the corps' air service) commenced P-72B operations, principally training missions conducted on behalf of the Centro Aviazione (the Aviation Centre and the hub of the training activities) at Pratica di Mare Air Base near Rome. The aim was to qualify instructors and pilots assigned to the Gruppo Esplorazione Aeromarittima (GEA, or Air Maritime Exploration Squadron) which reports to the Comando Operativo Aeronavale (Air Maritime Operational Command).

Pilot Training

GEA pilot training started in September 2019, more than two months before the delivery of the first aircraft. Initially the conversion programme involved instructor pilots and was subsequently extended to include pilots flying the ATR-42, dubbed the P-42A under the Italian military designation system.

Pilots already qualified on the ATR-42, undertook a shorter D course comprising seven simulator missions with ATR in Toulouse, France, followed by two missions flown from Pratica di Mare, and another three flights to gain operational qualification.

During 2020 training courses were disrupted due to the COVID-19 pandemic and overseas detachments were all cancelled given the mandatory quarantine requirements in the event of a positive test with any crew. Consequently, the Centro Aviazione conducted a D course in house and without the simulators with ATR in Toulouse. Pilots flew nine missions for type conversion, followed by a further three to gain operational qualification.

A different path was established for new pilots arriving directly from a flying school. Guardia di Finanza pilots undergo a screening phase with the Aeronautica Militare (Italian Air Force), flying the T-260B with 70° Stormo to gain their initial licence, followed by 18-months of multi-engine training with the US Navy to qualify as a military pilot. Back in Italy, pilots undertake a P-72B conversion course comprising 12 simulator missions with ATR at Toulouse, and two flights from Pratica di Mare. That amounts to 52 hours on type and gains the pilot type qualification on the P-72B. Operational qualification requires 24 missions for an approximate total of 48 hours.

All system operators and specialists are trained at the Centro Aviazione della Guardia di Finanza. A standard P-72B crew comprises two pilots, three systems operators, and two specialists, while a reinforced crew tasked for a long-range mission requires an additional pilot and two more system operators.

Mission Systems

P-72B mission avionics are based on the latest MS version of the Leonardo Airborne Tactical Observation System (ATOS MS), which according to the company offers varied functionality, such as the control and management of the mission systems, management of communications via satellite, 3G, LTE, file exchange, streaming video and internet navigation through the INMARSAT terminal and its associated router, the registration of images and video, mission planning based on the assigned task, and the documentation of the actual mission performed.

The ATOS MS system comprises a suite of active and passive sensors, communications, and a satellite communication system that include:
• The Gabbiano UL TS-80 radar, operating in the 9.0-10 GHz band. It offers capability to conduct surveillance over land with ground mapping, synthetic aperture radar and ground moving target indicator modes, and over water with sea surveillance, sea state monitoring, and navigation support functions. It is fundamental to the ATOS MS system. The radar's antenna is housed in a radome installed beneath the fuselage, affording 360° coverage in azimuth.
• A Wescam MX-20 imaging system is also positioned under the fuselage. The turret can rotate through 360° in azimuth, and between +30° and -120° in elevation. Cameras include daylight TV with a continuous zoom lens, infra-red TV with pre-established focal length zoom lens, plus a laser illuminator, and a laser range finder.
• An AIS (Automatic Identification System). An automatic inter-ship communication system operating in the mobile maritime VHF band. It can transmit and receive, can be used in receive mode only, and is obligatory equipment for all vessels over 300 tonnes. AIS is also used by many smaller boats, because it has proved to be a

LEFT • *Grifo 21, the second P-72B delivered to the Guardia di Finanza was initially operated in a green configuration.* GUARDIA DI FINANZA/MAJOR GIUSEPPE CASBARRA VIA AUTHOR

valid safety system. The AIS transmits information regarding the ship, its position, speed, identification, and other data. In the field of maritime surveillance and maritime rescue it enables the operators to immediately identify a ship, but also raise attention on those vessels which do not have it.
• An ASARS system for aviation search and rescue.
• An IMSI Catcher 2G/3G/4G system capable of capturing signals from mobile phones operating on GSM, UMTS and LTE networks.
• An IMSI Catcher IsatPhone/Thuraya, useful for identifying satellite users.
• Communications apparatus includes RT-700-1 and RT-700/F VHF/UHF radios, an NTX-138 VHF-FM radio and an INMARSAT voice/data system.

Cabin Layout

Like all multi-engine patrol aircraft, the P-72's internal layout comprises a flight deck and the aft cabin. The latter comprises an area dedicated to the tactical table with two operators, a central section with three mission consoles, a rear section configured with two observer positions featuring a hemispheric panoramic window on either side of the fuselage and seats for 16 passengers, and finally the tail, which houses, among other equipment, the hatch for the dropping of a life raft.

All three mission consoles are identical and allow the operator to

Leonardo P-72B Characteristics	
Wingspan	88ft 9in (27.05m)
Height	25ft 1in (7.65m)
Length	89ft 2in (27.17m)
Max take-off weight	50,700lb (23,000kg)
Cruise speed	280kts
Max range	1,780nm (1,500km)
Ceiling	25,000ft
Engines	Two Pratt & Whitney Canada PW127M turboprop engines each rated at 2,750shp (1,846kW)

Source: Leonardo

call up imagery fed from the various on-board sensors. Data fusion provides the maximum level of clarity and the greatest amount of information on one intuitive image.

During operations, one console is dedicated to monitoring the radar, one to the MX-20 imaging system and the third serves as a back-up, or for additional monitoring of one of the two systems.

P-72 Sentiments

According to Lieutenant Colonel Francesco Corcelli, commander of the GEA: "The avionics have been greatly improved and with them the capacities of the aircraft. Moreover, the P-72B offers a greater level of comfort for the crew and increased endurance, given that now it can fly for up to nine hours."

Discussing the development of the P-72B programme, Brigadier General Joselito Minuto, commander of the Guardia di Finanza's Centro di Aviazione said: "The third aircraft has a multi-spectral tele-imaging system produced by Canadian company ITRES. Two different sensors will be installed. A SAVI 1000 and TABI 1800, both integrated with a high-resolution camera. One sensor will be dedicated to the hyper-spectral field and the other to the thermic field, which will permit high-altitude monitoring of an area of land or ocean for the identification, for example, of narcotics cultivation or the burying or spill of noxious materials.

Tasking of the P-72B is, in the main, comprises long range patrol flights for detecting and monitoring ships suspected of illegal activity, and maritime search and rescue operations for people in difficulty at sea.

P-72s assigned to the GEA are heavily tasked with two types of mission: national missions, tasked directly by the corps, or those from an international organisation. For the latter, they usually support the European Border and Coast Guard Agency, FRONTEX, by conducting missions patrolling international areas of ocean. The Guardia di Finanza undertakes mission planning with the international coordination centre located at Pratica di Mare. Others included surveillance missions around Greece and the Eastern Mediterranean of the frontier with Turkey, and in the Western Mediterranean. All such missions involve the search and rescue of refugees, and migrants at sea, monitoring of terrorist activity and infiltration, and trafficking of narcotics.

A New Leader

Mark Ayton reviews the brand-new single-engine Beechcraft Denali

Prior to announcing the Beechcraft Model 220 Denali, Textron Aviation offered 18 different aircraft types ranging from the Cessna Skyhawk to the large Citation Longitude business jet. Despite this broad product range, Textron Aviation did not have a single engine, high-performance turboprop to compete with the Pilatus PC-12. To fill that gap, the company announced the Denali, a clean sheet design aircraft with no inclusion of components from any other Textron Aviation aircraft. The Denali aircraft, McCauley propeller and GE Aviation Catalyst engine are currently going through their respective certification process.

Aircraft features include:

- A large cargo door measuring 32in (W) x 51in (H) with gas-filled struts for opening and electric motor assistance to lower the door.
- A robust trailing link landing gear capable of operating from unimproved runways.
- Fixed steps to allow passenger entry onboard.
- A digitally controlled pressurisation system with a 6,000ft cabin pressure up to 31,000ft which provides a comfortable cabin ideal for the medical evacuation role.
- A six-seat interior comprising a club four arrangement in the forward part of the cabin, two forward-facing aft seats, or a commuter style layout with nine forward-facing seats with recline, cupholders and a USB port at each seat.
- A choice of two different lavatories in the back: a carry-on lavatory with a door and bulkhead for privacy or a permanently plumbed in externally-serviced lavatory.
- The six-seat interior features a refreshment unit featuring storage drawers, containers, trash containers and a garment hanger positioned forward of the seats.
- An alternate combi configuration with the club four seat arrangement in the forward part and space for freight with the aft seats removed.
- A square oval fuselage cross section that enables a comfortable seated position with good headroom above each seat and a flat floor which makes walking around the cabin easy.
- Winglets to reduce drag.
- A digital weather radar housed in a pod mounted on the right-side wing-tip. The radar scans the weather ahead and displays the weather pattern on an MFD to help the pilots avoid inclement weather for a smoother ride.
- A starter generator and a backup generator both fitted on the engine for redundancy, and back-up batteries.
- A magneto provides electrical power for the engine FADEC if electrical power and battery power are both lost.
- Glass triple-pane electrically heated windshields.

BELOW • *A computer generated image of a Denali showing the winglets and the wing tip pod housing the weather radar on the right wing.* TEXTRON AVIATION

- Four 16in diameter passenger windows on each side.
- A cabin that features pockets on the sidewalls for tablets, power outlets, and USB ports.
- LED lighting throughout the aircraft.

Maintenance

Textron Aviation designed the Denali with a task-based inspection programme at 800 hours between checks and some components with an 18-month inspection interval. By design, components are all accessible for maintenance purposes housed behind large access panels secured by latches rather than screws for easy access, which helps to bring down the cost of maintenance and operation.

Unique amongst Textron Aviation's newest aircraft are 3DPubs, which provide interactive step-by-step procedural instructions to help maintenance technicians review and validate processes virtually before working on an aircraft. Using a colour-coding system, technicians can quickly differentiate visuals to identify line replacement units, hardware, discarded parts, sealant application areas and specialised tools.

A Brand-New Engine

The Catalyst engine, a product of Avio Aero, part of GE Aerospace, was developed at its facilities in the Czech Republic, Germany, Italy and Poland. Its architecture and technologies are based on the GE T700 engine, powerplant of the UH-60 Blackhawk and AH-64 Apache helicopters, which is proven in high-cycle operations and harsh environments, with millions of hours of accumulated flight time.

Much of the engine's aerodynamic design comes from GE Aerospace's engineering expertise on large commercial engines, including liquid-cooled turbine technology and use of hollow blades.

Cool air passes through the hollow blades to prevent them from overheating and stretching while running the engine at hot, more efficient temperatures.

The Catalyst engine completed its first flight in September 2021 on Beechcraft King Air 300 testbed OK-CTU (c/n FL-276). The Catalyst engine was fitted on the left side to flight test the turboprop and work through its certification process. The privately owned testbed was based at Berlin-Brandenburg Airport.

Textron Aviation's decision to opt for a brand-new engine for the Denali was driven by the desire to introduce newer technologies to the marketplace. Explaining, Martin Tuck, a senior

technical marketing advisor with Textron Aviation said: "The company issued bids and GE Aerospace gave a very convincing argument for producing a brand new 21st century engine that meets all the latest emission regulations."

The Catalyst Engine

According to GE Aerospace, the Catalyst engine is the first all-new, clean-sheet engine designed and produced for the turboprop market in more than 50 years.

During its development, GE Aerospace utilised technologies proven on the company's large commercial engines which have amassed millions of flight hours to balance the all-new design with lower risk.

The Catalyst engine features pilot-friendly, full-authority integrated digital engine and propeller control, which automatically optimises fuel flow, prop pitch and speed, bleed valves and variable inlet stators for maximum efficiency in all conditions.

It is the world's first turboprop engine featuring 3-D printed components, which are claimed to be both lighter and more durable and ultimately deliver the best power-to-weight ratio in the engine's class. This also provides increased range, added payload, and an improved passenger experience thanks to the larger, quieter cabin.

According to GE Aerospace, the Catalyst engine reduces CO_2 emissions and results in up to 20% lower

Beechcraft 220 Denali Flight-Test Aircraft

Aircraft	Registration and c/n	Test activity
Prototype	N220BT (c/n E220-744001) made the type's first flight on November 22, 2021, from Eisenhower International Airport, Wichita. Piloted by senior test pilot Peter Gracey and chief test pilot Dustin Smisor, they completed a 2hrs 50mins flight and tested the aircraft's performance, stability, and control, as well as its propulsion, environmental, flight controls and avionics systems. The aircraft reached an altitude of 15,600ft and attained speeds of 180kts.	Uniquely configured for flight envelope expansion, aerodynamic, and performance testing. As required for such testing it was fitted with a tail chute for stall testing.
Pre-production aircraft P1	N221NT (c/n 220-0001) first flew on June 16, 2022, from Eisenhower International Airport, Wichita. During the 2hrs 1min flight, the aircraft reached an altitude of 15,500ft with a max speed of 240kts.	Primarily engine, avionics and systems integration testing.
Pre-production aircraft P2	N222NT (c/n 220-0002) first flew in September 2022.	P2 is a passenger-configured aircraft with a full up interior. P2 is used for interior, environmental, and human factor engineering testing.

fuel consumption. Additive technology has been used in combination with advanced alloys to enable more advanced component designs and a reduced part count. This reduction in complexity allows more geometrical freedom in its design, reduces weight and fuel burn.

Notable features of the Catalyst engine are:

- A propeller gearbox which uses a planetary gear arrangement to transfer power generated by the power turbine to the propeller, featuring an additive-made casing.
- A power turbine that features three stages and a 3D aerodynamic design to maximise the power extraction and efficiency across the entire flight envelope.
- A combustor that's compact, with reverse flow design and advanced fuel nozzles which enables more complete combustion to reduce emissions and visible exhaust soot.
- A compressor that's compact, with a four-stage, axial, single centrifugal design which provides a class-leading 16:1 pressure ratio yielding unrivalled efficiency and power.
- A control system which commands engine and propeller operations and enables single lever power and significantly reduces pilot workload.

GE Aerospace claims:

- The Catalyst engine is engineered to perform with the same level of dispatch reliability as its engines used on current passenger aircraft.
- With over 900 million flight hours of FADEC experience, its dual-channel, full-authority digital engine and propeller control offer pilots enhanced responsiveness, optimised performance, and simplified flying.
- The compact compressor module delivers a class-leading 16:1 pressure ratio, and its high-pressure efficiency yields lower specific fuel consumption in all phases of flight.
- The compact reverse-flow combustor, advanced fuel nozzles and reduced fuel burn are not only efficient, but also eco-friendly. The Catalyst engine is designed to deliver greater reductions in emissions and soot compared to other engines in its class.
- The integrated propulsion control system automatically optimises fuel flow, prop pitch and speed, bleed valves, and variable stators for maximum efficiency in all conditions.
- The propellor blade's internal cooling passages allow the blades to run at higher temperatures, resulting in greater efficiency.

Garmin 3000 Integrated Flight Deck

Prior to the launch of the Beechcraft Denali, Textron Aviation used the Garmin G3000 integrated flight deck on the Cessna Citation M2 Gen2 and CJ3+ business jets.

The basic architecture of the G3000 system installed on the Denali is essentially the same, with slight differences. The Denali G3000 flight deck comes as standard with three 14.1in WXGA high-resolution displays used as either a primary flight display (PFD) or multifunction display (MFD) – or in

LEFT • *Garmin's G3000 Integrated Flight Deck.* TEXTRON AVIATION

reversionary mode as both.

According to Garmin: "When used as the pilot's PFD, the wider screen provides more visual area for the simulated 3-D perspective topography of Garmin's Synthetic Vision Technology – as well as enhanced peripheral cues from an extended horizon line. Using the G3000's terrain alerting database to create a detailed graphical landscape, the SVT provides a virtual reality perspective view of ground and water features, obstacles, and traffic – all shown in relative proximity to the aircraft. Instead of a flat blue-over-brown representation, the pilots see a realistic visual depiction of flight data. So, they can picture what lies beyond the nose of their aircraft, even in solid IFR or night-time/marginal VFR conditions. In addition, a large inset map allows more traffic and terrain/obstacles data to be accommodated on the PFD for even better situational awareness."

The displays are arranged three-abreast, one each as a PFD for the pilot and co-pilot, and a central MFD. Two glass touchscreen GTC 575 controllers are located two-abreast at the upper portion of the central pedestal immediately below the centre MFD. The GTC 575 controller serves as the pilot's primary point of entry for the G3000 system. It features a desktop-style, icon-driven interface built on a shallow menu structure. The GTC 575 enables the pilot to access more systems and sensors with fewer keystrokes or page sequences via icon-identified touch keys on the controller. This makes functions easy to locate and access with fewer hand/

eye movements in the cockpit.

In addition to full NAV/COMM radio management and simplified page navigation on the MFD, the pilot can also use the 5.7in high-resolution GTC 575 screen to control the remote audio/intercom system, transponder codes and idents, electronic checklist entries, flight plan entry and editing, plus optional synoptic data and other selected mapping, traffic, weather, entertainment, and custom display options.

Handy BACK and HOME keys on the display let the pilot quickly retrace steps or return to the desktop from any page – so they never get lost in the software or need to memorise lengthy user sequences.

The GTC retains a single set of mechanical concentric knobs, along with a volume control knob and dedicated map joystick. If the pilot prefers, the dual knobs can be used in lieu of the touchscreen to enter frequencies for selected radios or to toggle between Comm 1 and 2. The current function of these knobs is always clearly identified in the touchscreen window above them. The centre MFD enables two separate vertical pages to be viewed side-by-side – along with the aircraft's EIS strip for engine and fuel data. This split-screen functionality enables the pilot to pair, say, the airway chart and the approach plate, or the satellite weather and flight planning pages.

Graphical synoptics for airframe, electrical and fuel systems offer easier monitoring and faster troubleshooting. The high-aspect-ratio displays allow enhanced viewing and management of multiple sensor inputs – making the MFD more multi-functional. ✈

Beechcraft 220 Denali Characteristics

Length	48ft 9in (14.86m)
Height	15ft 3in (4.65m)
Wingspan	54ft 3in (16.54m)
Full fuel payload	1,100lb (499kg)
Max cruise speed	285kts (528km/h)
Max range	1,600nm (2,963km)
Take-off distance	Under 3,000ft (914m)
Max operating altitude	31,000ft (9,449m)
Cabin height	4ft 10in (1.47m)
Cabin width	5ft 3in (1.60m)
Cabin length	16ft 9in (5.11m)
Cargo door	4ft 4in (W) x 4ft 3in (H)
	1.32m (W) x 1.30m (H)
Max occupants	8-11
Propellor	McCauley Blackmac heavy-duty five-blade carbon fibre propeller fitted with metal leading edge guards, scimitar tips, and electric-powered boots for ice protection, which is digitally controlled with reversible pitch. Overhaul interval set at 6,000 hours.

Source: Textron Aviation

RIGHT • *The club four seating arrangement in the forward part of the Denali's cabin.* TEXTRON AVIATION

ABOVE • *Denali prototype N220BT on its November 22, 2021, maiden flight from Eisenhower International Airport, Wichita.* TEXTRON AVIATION

The entire flight deck layout is designed to single pilot operations with everything within easy reach of the pilot's left seat.

The narrow centre pedestal, below the two touchscreen controllers, houses the power lever which has a Garmin integrated auto throttle as standard. Flap control is positioned on the right side, and electric aileron and rudder trim controls near the bottom.

Landing Gear

The Denali is equipped with a rugged trailing-link clean sheet design landing gear and large tyres to aid smooth landings. In terms of its trailing link design, it's like the landing gear used by the Cessna Citation XLS business jet.

The Denali landing gear comprises the main strut, a retraction/extension actuator, a locking actuator, locking links, a diagonal side stay, and a trailing arm with a pivot point in front of the wheel which allows the wheel to hinge up and down to absorb and dissipate the kinetic energy of landing impact.

The Beechcraft Denali is an all-electric aircraft, so it does not use a dedicated hydraulic system to drive the flaps or landing gear actuation. This simplifies maintenance, reduces the cost of operation and is more environmentally friendly because it does not require hydraulic fluid for the systems other than the brakes.

The landing gears comprise a stainless-steel main landing gear which retracts inward into the wings and a nose landing gear that retracts aft into the fuselage nose. Each leg supports a single tyre. The main gear is a trailing link design which results in good cushioning for even the heaviest of landings.

The landing gear handle on the flight deck commands the landing gear actuators to retract or extend depending on the lever position. The landing gear LOCKED depiction (three greens when down and locked) is shown on the MFD below the engine indications. Flap position indication is also shown in the same location.

For emergency extension, the Denali uses a conventional nitrogen gas blow-down system.

Flight Testing and Certification

The Denali flight test programme

involves three aircraft, a prototype and two pre-production aircraft, P1 and P2, each designed to do different things, details are listed in table on p28.

Textron Aviation also developed the iron bird, a Denali avionics and systems test rig, used to run tests on a particular system, and if required, to refine the whole system before its flown and tested on an aircraft. The auto throttle setting is one example.

The rig has all the necessary controls and servos in place, so when a pilot makes an input into the controls, it feels like they are flying the aircraft. It's not a full functioning simulator that moves, but it does allow the pilot to test out different systems before they fly with the system under test on an aircraft. One system currently under test with the

rig is the latest upgrade of the Garmin G3000 flight deck in preparation for its installation on a Denali test aircraft.

Prototype

The prototype aircraft is used for early envelope expansion, early aerodynamic testing, stability, control and its performance for example speed and altitude. Early events included reaching the maximum operating altitude of 31,000 feet, stalls at different altitudes, and take-off and landing characteristics.

Explaining, Textron Aviation engineering flight test pilot, Dustin Smisor said: "Proto gives us a first look at how the aircraft works, what it feels like, and how the flight controls operate. During 2023, we will look more heavily at the performance of the aircraft so things like cruise performance, take-off, and landing performance, and flying performance. With Proto we learn how the aircraft handles in extreme parts of the envelope that we wouldn't test using aircraft P1 or P2."

Pre-Production Aircraft P1

P1 is dedicated to systems integration primarily with the engine.

Smisor described P1 as: "Our systems test article. We take a deep dive at how things like the engine works, how the environmental control system works, how the landing gear system works, etc."

To gain insight into how the engine and systems hold up against harsh situations, P1 is tested in extreme hot and cold conditions. P1 recently faced intense heat in Yuma, Arizona, testing systems in high temperatures. Testing

against the heat will continue but P1 will eventually travel to more frigid climates to analyse the systems against extreme cold. Relying on natural weather is ideal, but if it's not available P1 will fly to Eglin Air Force Base in Florida, where the McKinley Climatic Laboratory allows for simulated conditions. Smisor noted that while most aircraft may never see conditions like these, it is important to understand what the aircraft can handle. "The testing takes us to the extremes of the envelope to verify that the systems such as the fuel system, the engine, the electrical system, avionics, brakes, all of those systems continue to work well in those cold and hot environments," he said.

Pre-Production Aircraft P2

P2 represents what the final product could be fitted with including a full interior.

Explaining P2's role in the test programme, Smisor said: "We are designing to make this aircraft the best in its class in terms of the room in the interior, the layout, and the style. I think as the team installed that interior, they learned some things about how they can sequence that and make it more efficient."

With heavy emphasis on the Garmin G3000 avionics suite, P2 has also seen milestones including having an interior fit for configuration. Smisor said the use of customer feedback has been important in developing P2. Explaining, he said: "While it may only seem like seats or window shades to some, the significance of this process mirrors the others. It takes a lot of effort and time, but it is well worth it because it is a learning process and because you can say this is the finished product. Now you can look at how the air conditioning works, how the heater works, what the noise level is, how it feels and looks in the back for our customer. It is multi-purpose and very useful in a lot of areas."

At the time of writing in late February, 2023 the three aircraft had amassed 950 hours of flight-test time, and P1 and P2 were in northern Canada conducting cold weather testing including engine stops and battery efficiency.

Another King

Mark Ayton reviews the latest variants of the ubiquitous
Beechcraft King Air.

I n its brief write-up of the King Air's history, Textron Aviation says: "After designing and manufacturing piston and jet engine aircraft, Walter Beech's namesake company, then Beech Aircraft, developed a compromise between the two – the King Air. It was the perfect middle ground between the other two segments, flying faster and higher than the piston aircraft while also encompassing the capability to land at small airports on short runways. From 1964 on, the King Air family

of turboprops outsold all its twin-turboprop competitors combined.

"It began with the Beechcraft Model 90 King Air which seated six to eight people with a 270mph cruising speed, above weather capability and the ability to land on small fields and airstrips. In just 90 days after the aircraft was first announced, Beech Aircraft had accepted orders totalling $10.8 million. After first flight, orders and deposits totalled more than $12 million and demand began to outgrow supply. Beech delivered 100 of the original King Air by 1966 and 400 by 1968. After five

years Beech introduced the King Air 100 to its aircraft line-up, followed by the A100 and B100 variants followed in 1972 and 1979 respectively.

"Beech developed the Model 200 Super King Air which first flew on October 27, 1972. It was the first T-tail configured King Air produced after four years of research and development. The new tail was raised above the wing's downwash, allowing the stabilizer and elevator to operate in relatively smooth, undisturbed air. This configuration set the standard for future King Air turboprops and is still seen on King Air aircraft today.

Aside from the business and utility sectors, King Air turboprops are widely used for specialized missions including aerial survey, air ambulance and surveillance.

"The squared oval cabin cross-section allows for a variety of customizable configurations and the capability to land where many other aircraft cannot. The latest variants are the Model 260 and the Model 360."

King Air 260

Certified to FAA Part 23 standard as single pilot operable and a maximum take-off weight of 12,500lb, means the King Air 260 does not require an FAA or EASA type rating. This is beneficial for the operator because it does not require as much burdensome training compared to a King Air 360 which requires any pilot to maintain a type rating.

As part of the upgrade from King Air 250 to King Air 260, a Textron Aviation design team created a modern interior for the 260. Its predecessor, the King Air 250 had not undergone an interior re-design in several years. Explaining, the builder's senior technical marketing advisor, Alex Hunt said: "We've re-sculpted all the cabinetry, using real wood veneers throughout the cabin, and improved the refreshment centre. The cabin seats were also re-designed using digital pressure mapping. Dozens of people sat on a seat with embedded sensors to map out how each different body type puts pressure onto a seat. This enables design of a seat structure and a foam design that accommodates all body types. The seats can move

in four directions and have adjustable headrests and armrests."

Textron designers uses a club configuration in which seats face each other, which gained two inches of additional legroom over the King Air 250.

"More importantly, there are two additional aft facing seats positioned immediately aft of the flight deck with six inches of additional legroom. While the seats have always been comfortable, legroom in the AFT facing seats has been challenging."

The cabin is equipped with USB charging points, soft lighting, and dual zone temperature control so the cockpit and cabin temperatures can be controlled independently, which is beneficial to pilots and passengers.

According to Alex, the King Air 260 and 360 are considered to have quiet cabins: "Beechcraft engineers devised a solution called tune dynamic vibration absorbers to help lower the cabin volume significantly. There are 32 absorbers installed on a 260 and over 100 on a 360. This is a passive system that's tuned to the specific frequency of the propeller and engine. It absorbs the vibrational energy that humans pick up as volume or a sound, and significantly reduces the cabin noise throughout the entire aircraft. There's no electricity and no maintenance, they just vibrate in the sidewall."

ThrustSense Auto Throttle

Textron introduced the IS&S ThrustSense full regime auto throttle as standard on both the King Air 260 and King Air 360. The auto throttle enables a pilot to dial in a speed or torque

setting. The auto throttle system will automatically compute and control the appropriate power lever levels to suit the phase of flight.

Servos housed in the throttle quadrant directly move the throttle levers to maintain the appropriate power. This enables the pilot to set the take-off torque and instead of monitoring the engines to prevent over torquing, the pilot can look down the runway during take-off.

A unique feature of the auto throttle is an envelope protection mode called Lifeguard that operates during critical phases of flight. In the unlikely event of a loss of an engine during take-off the auto throttle would automatically adjust the power of the operating engine to keep it within the controllability limits. It gives the pilot enough power to climb away from the ground, maintain a climb gradient to an altitude and diagnose the issue without providing a power level that would overpower the rudder. During this critical phase of flight, Lifeguard does a lot of the work for the pilot so they can focus on flying the aeroplane to a safe altitude.

The King Air 260 has an upgraded pressurisation system that improves passenger comfort and reduces pilot workload. The digital pressurisation controller hosted within the flight management system automatically meets the requirements of the cabin pressurisation schedule on climb and in descent. It pressurises the aircraft early in the take-off sequence, which eliminates pressurisation bumps encountered when the aircraft catches up in flight.

The King Air 260 is powered by the Pratt & Whitney Canada PT6A-52 engine (as per the 250) whereas the King Air 360 is powered the Pratt & Whitney Canada PT6A-60A (as per the 350).

Take-off performance is another differentiator between the 260 and the 360. Beechcraft specifies 2,111ft for the 260 and 3,300ft for the 360. But the specified distances are based on different criteria. The 2,111ft take-off distance specified for the 260 is required to safely clear a 50ft obstacle whereas the 3,300ft take-off distance specified for the 360 is a balanced field length which accounts for an engine failure at a critical moment as the aircraft starts to rotate with enough runway length remaining to stop.

The latest versions of the Beechcraft King Air, a 260 LEFT and a 360 RIGHT. TEXTRON AVIATION

King Air 360

The King Air 360 is certified to Part 23 category standards as single pilot operable, but requires a type rating given its 15,000lb max take-off weight.

A King Air 360 is 2ft 10in (0.8m) longer than the 260, flies 2kts faster and costs $2 less per hour to operate than a 260.

The 360 seats nine passengers in the cabin because of a double club configuration, the 260 seats seven.

With the double club configuration, the four seats that fit back-to-back midship have what Beechcraft calls a midship pyramid cabinet between them.

The cabin is fitted with accent lighting throughout (as is the 260) and lower air and light adjusters to prevent passengers from striking their head despite maximised space around the head and shoulders area provided by the square-oval cabin cross section with a vertical height of 57in (1.45m).

Unique to the King Air 360 are wing lockers, each with a 300lb stowage capacity, typically used for inlet plugs, prop slings and similar, which can be loaded asymmetrically.

As their predecessors, both the 260 and 360 are equipped with winglets which improve the aircraft's aspect ratio, reduces drag and wingtip vortices.

When configured as an air ambulance, the King Air 360 accommodates two powered life

Beechcraft King Air 360 and King Air 260 Characteristics

	King Air 360	King Air 260
Length	46ft 8in (14.22m)	43ft 10in (13.36m)
Height	14ft 4in (4.37m)	14ft 10in (4.52m)
Wingspan	57ft 11in (17.65m)	57ft 11in (17.65m)
Wing area	310ft2 (28.8m^2)	310ft2 (28.8m^2)
Wheelbase	16ft 3in (4.95m)	14ft 11in (4.55m)
Tread	17ft 2in (5.23m)	17ft 2in (5.23m)
Max ramp weight	15,100lb (6.849kg)	12,590lb (5,711kg)
Max take-off weight	15,000lb (6,804kg)	12,500lb (5,670kg)
Usable fuel weight	3,611lb (1,638kg)	3,645lb (1,653kg)
Usable fuel volume	539 US gal (2,040lit)	544 US gal (2,059lit)
Empty weight	9,955lb (4,516kg)	8,830lb (4,005kg)
Useful load	5,145lb (2,334kg)	3,760lb (1,706kg)
Max payload	2,545lb (1,154kg)	2,170lb (984kg)
Max cruise speed	312kts (578kph)	310kts (574kph)
Max range	1,806nm (3,345km)	1,720nm (3,185km)
Take-off distance	3,300ft (1,006m) field length	2,111ft (643m) take-off disrtance over a 50ft obstacle
Max operating altitude	35,000ft (10,668m)	35,000ft (10,668m)
Cabin height	57in (1.45m)	57in (1.45m)
Cabin width	54in (1.37m)	54in (1.37m)
Cabin length	19ft 6in (5.94m)	16ft 8in (5.08m)
Cargo door (optional)	52in (W) x 52in (H) 1.32m (W) x 1.32m (H) Opens upward with clearance below that enables medics to easily load medical equipment.	52in (W) x 52in (H) 1.32m (W) x 1.32m (H) Opens upward with clearance below that enables medics to easily load medical equipment.
Internal baggage capacity	550lb (249kg)	550lb (249kg)
Internal baggage volume	55.3ft3 (1.57m^3)	55.3ft3 (1.57m^3)
Wing locker capacity	Two lockers each with 300lb (136kg) capacity	Not applicable
Max occupants	11	9
Powerplant	Two Pratt & Whitney Canada PT6A-60A each rated at 1,050shp (783kW)	Two Pratt & Whitney Canada PT6A-52A each rated at 850shp (634kW) Both engine variants provide adequate power in harsh hot and high conditions.
Propellor	Hartzell four-blade aluminium constant-speed auto-feathering propeller.	Hartzell four-blade aluminium constant-speed auto-feathering propeller.

Source: Textron Aviation

RIGHT • *This shot of a King Air 260 clearly shows the Hartzell four-blade aluminium constant-speed auto-feathering propellors.* TEXTRON AVIATION

TOP • *The Collins Aerospace Proline Fusion integrated flight deck.* TEXTRON AVIATION

BELOW • *Winglets fitted to the latest King Air models help to reduce drag, increase fuel economy and airspeed.* TEXTRON AVIATION

support units. Seat tracks installed on the ceiling allow defibrillators, monitors, and support equipment to be appropriately positioned, and the length of the patient area to be adjusted to suit.

King Air 360 Standard Features

- IS&S ThrustSense full regime auto throttle lessens the pilot's workload and provides some envelope protection for increased safety.
- An enhanced automated digital pressurisation system with a lower cabin altitude which is simpler to manage than the King Air's previous pressurisation controller operated by the pilot.
- Digital pressurisation indication.
- Collins Aerospace Pro Line Fusion avionics suite.
- Three 14in touchscreen displays.
- Synthetic vision.
- Graphical flight planning.
- Integrated charts and maps.
- Engine indicating and crew alerting system.
- Dual flight management system.
- Fully-automated, multi-scan weather radar system optimised for short-, mid- and long-range weather (also equips the King Air 260).
- Integrated terrain awareness and warning system (ITAWS).
- Two traffic alert and collision avoidance (TCAS II) systems: TCAS I is standard on the King Air 260.
- Automatic flight guidance system (AFGS).
- Dual navigation and communication radios.

Pro Line Fusion Integrated Flight Deck

Both the King Air 260 and the 360 feature the Collins Aerospace Pro Line Fusion avionics suite, an upgrade from the former Pro Line 21 suite. The Pro Line Fusion suite has features usually found on larger aircraft with a lot of redundancy built in, for example dual flight management systems.

The integrated flight deck features three 14in touch-control primary flight displays (the main difference between the two systems) which enable pilots to interact with the displays, integrated head-up high-resolution synthetic vision systems, graphical touch-screen flight planning, convenient pre-sets to reconfigure all three displays with a single touch, full multi-sensor

flight management system, touch screen checklists, open and scalable architecture for future upgrades and mandates, and precision GPS capabilities.

Synthetic vision is standard. It provides pilots with a database-driven view of outside the aircraft, which improves a pilot's situational awareness.

The pilot can control all flight deck features using either a touchscreen or by one of the two controllers located on the centre pedestal. A pilot uses a cursor control device (like a joystick) to move the target around the screen.

According to Alex Hunt, King Air pilots tend to use a touchscreen or a controller during different phases of flight. "We find that during start-up and taxi, pilots tend to use the touchscreens more, but then in flight, most pilots use a centre pedestal mounted controller."

In addition to touchscreens and controllers, the flight deck is also equipped with a QWERTY keyboard which enables the pilot to quickly input information into the FMS, and a system called Quick tune which enables the pilot to quickly tune the radio. Explaining, Alex said: "If the tower says contact departure on 134.8, the pilot can just type in 348, click the quick tune button and it recognises the entry as a frequency and enters the leading digit. Or if the pilot enters 5045, it recognises that as a transponder code, and will automatically tune the IFF to that squawk code. Both features reduce pilot workload a little bit, which is especially useful, especially in busy airspace."

The Multitasker

Mark Ayton reviews the all-American Cessna C208 Grand Caravan.

Cessna delivered the first of its Model 208 Caravan turboprop aircraft on February 25, 1985. The customer was an air service provider based in Alaska which preceded the first aircraft delivery to a FedEx feeder operator.

Today the FedEx feeder network is a strategic component of the overall global linehaul network, serving markets too small for direct FedEx Express air linehaul service. The feeder network uses nearly 300 aircraft with a maximum gross take-off weight under 60,000lb and serves over 250 locations around the world. FedEx feeder aircraft include ATR 42s, ATR 72s, Cessna SkyCouriers, and Caravans. FedEx remains one of the biggest Caravan operators over 40 years after the company's involvement in the type's development. The prototype's maiden flight took place on December 9, 1982, followed by FAA type certification in October 1984.

According to Textron Aviation's senior technical marketing advisor Alex Hunt the big differences between the Cessna Model 208 Caravan and the Model 208B Grand Caravan are a shorter fuselage, the engine (the Caravan is powered by the PT6-114A rated at 675shp), and range. The Caravan can fly further than the EX because its lower horsepower engine burns less fuel.

Grand Caravan

In 1986, the Wichita-based company received FAA type-certification for the Model 208B Grand Caravan, a Model 208 with a 4ft longer fuselage in freighter configuration.

Development of the Grand Caravan was driven by Caravan operator requirements who were bulking out in volume terms rather than weight. Generally, a package contains a small component in a large box: it doesn't weigh much but it takes up a lot of volume. According to Alex Hunt the extra cabin volume provided by the extended fuselage satisfies the volume requirement of many operators.

The first Grand Caravan 208B was delivered in 1990. The two models have sold well, Cessna delivered the 1,000th production Caravan 208 in 1998 and the 1,000th Grand Caravan 208B in 2002.

In 2008, Cessna certified the Grand Caravan with the Garmin G1000 all-glass avionics suite as the standard system. According to Garmin, the G1000 makes flight information easier to scan and process, affording the pilot a greater level of situational awareness, simplicity, and safety in the cockpit. The glass flightdeck presents flight instrumentation, navigation, weather, terrain, traffic and engine data on large-format, high-resolution displays. Its flat-panel LCD displays are interchangeable for use as either a primary flight display or multi-function display.

Grand Caravan EX

The Grand Caravan's evolution continued and in 2012, Cessna introduced the Grand Caravan EX, a do-all, carry-all aircraft with lower acquisition and operating costs.

N594EX

RIGHT • *A Cessna Grand Caravan EX kicks up dirt on an unprepared runway.* TEXTRON AVIATION

The EX is powered by the Pratt & Whitney Canada PT6A-140 turboprop engine rated at 867shp (647kW) which entered service with the type. It provides almost 200shp more than the PT6A-114A engine introduced as standard on new build Caravans in 1998.

The first Grand Caravan EX was delivered in 2013, the same year the amphibian version received FAA type-certification after which deliveries commenced.

Because Cessna aircraft are widely operated, industry partners around the world continue to invest money to develop supplemental type certificates (STCs) for an aircraft such as a Grand Caravan. Textron Aviation can build an aircraft on the Wichita production line with provisions for those modifications and send the aircraft to its service centre to acquire the necessary STCs and install them.

According to Jens Torell, Textron Aviation's capabilities development manager for special mission aircraft: "Depending on the customer's schedule, they can send the aircraft to whatever STC holder they or Textron Aviation has identified as the right partner, so the aircraft can be delivered in its baseline configuration, with all modifications undertaken by the partner company under a separate contract. It's really tailored to the purchasing process, not just the aircraft's operating requirements. We work with governments and sometimes must tailor the purchasing vehicle on the contract to how the government does business. When a government has issued a formal request for proposal, the documentation provides a detailed outline of its air ambulance operation requirements. That's how we go about modifying the aircraft.

"Customer specification is driven by more than just the acquisition cost and includes the all-important capability. In the case of a turboprop aircraft like the Grand Caravan EX, its utility and austere capability for operating from remote rough runways are favourable."

Garmin G1000 NXi Integrated Flight Deck

The Grand Caravan EX is equipped with the Garmin G1000 NXi, the latest variant with improved processor speeds and faster memory which boots up significantly faster than the original G1000 system. The NXi features three 10in flat-panel LCD display units which are configured as dual PFDs and an MFD in the middle.

Two unique features of the NXi are a new dual audio panel featuring standard audio panels in front of both the pilot and the co-pilot who can independently tune their radio. The second is the Garmin Flight Steam 510 memory card which works with the Garmin Pilot or ForeFlight app loaded on a compatible smart device to wirelessly stream data to/from the avionics, saving the pilot time and workload in the cockpit. For example, Flight Stream 510 allows the pilot to do all flight planning on an iPad using an app. This enables the pilot to wirelessly connect the device to the cockpit and upload the flight plan or an update to the NXi avionics. The avionics in turn will transmit traffic and weather information back to the iPad.

A terrain avoidance and warning system and an enhanced automatic flight control system (AFCS) are options available with the NXi.

LEFT • *The ubiquitous Cessna 208 Grand Caravan EX.* TEXTRON AVIATION

Alex Hunt described the AFCS as: "an angel watching over your shoulder on every flight. It enhances the auto pilot by preventing the pilot from pitching or rolling outside of the normal flight envelopes by invoking a correction back to a

normal operating envelope. It also features under speed protection and coupled go around."

According to Garmin, with WAAS GPS-based guidance, the autopilot can fly coupled holding patterns, curved-path radius-to-fix legs, precision, and non-precision approaches, and coupled go-arounds.

The Grand Caravan EX can also be equipped with Garmin's SurfaceWatch runway identification and alerting technology, Connext wireless cockpit connectivity, horizontal situational indicator mapping displayed on a PFD, and animated weather radar via datalink.

Both the Caravan and the Grand Caravan EX provide pilots and passenger with easier entry than the original design. The aircraft have large pilot and co-pilot doors on each side, each with a boarding ladder. Passengers board through a door on the right-hand side fitted with a self-contained boarding stair. Located on the aft left-hand side of the aircraft, the cargo aircraft is big enough to load a full pallet directly from a forklift.

Both the Caravan and the Grand Caravan can carry a cargo pod fitted to the underside of the fuselage. The pod is a standard fit for freight operators such as the Fedex Feeder aircraft and is often taken as an option by owner-operators.

Some privately owned Caravans and Grand Caravan EXs carry a circular aerodynamic fairing fitted to the underside of the mid fuselage, it houses a tank that contains anti-icing fluid and is typically housed in the cargo pod. The fairing cannot carry bags or cargo.

Caravans and Grand Caravan EXs do not have a standard interior layout, an aspect driven by the customer's choice. Whatever the seating arrangement, the interior usually comprises an airline style configuration, but some owner operators opt for an interior akin to a business jet with plush seats, sidewalls, and tables.

The landing gear is of a spring steel design made of a unique alloy that does not retract. The landing gear strut absorbs the shock induced upon landing.

TOP LEFT • *Vietnam-based Hai Au Aviation operates amphibious Cessna Grand Caravan aircraft in various roles.* TEXTRON AVIATION

LEFT • *The Garmin G1000NXi integrated flight deck.* TEXTRON AVIATION

BELOW • *Cabin and cargo pod doors open on a Grand Caravan EX.* TEXTRON AVIATION

Textron Aviation assumes different roles in the procurement process for air ambulance aircraft. Sometimes another company acts as prime for the procurement contract, under which all it needs from Textron Aviation is the aircraft, and it assumes responsibility for the modifications. Often, government health system procurements involve leasing from a company that staff, own and operate the aircraft on behalf of the government. The company buys the aircraft direct from Textron Aviation and handles the completion process to fulfil the contract.

Flight controls are mechanically actuated, the flaps use an electric motor.

Icing Protection

One option offered by Cessna is a system known as FIKI or Flight Into Known Icing. Cessna has offered the TKS system since 2008. It features 800 laser-drilled holes per square inch on the leading edge of the tail, the wings, and in the strut. The system also features a windshield spray bar and has a 20-gallon tank to hold the TKS fluid. In normal mode the fluid lasts for over 200 minutes, 80 minutes in high mode, and just 40 minutes when the aircraft is picking up a lot of icing.

Explaining, Alex Hunt said: "This capable system allows you to fly into some of the toughest and most challenging conditions out there. If you don't have an icing system installed, you're not allowed to fly into air masses where the airframe will pick up ice because you have no way to rid the aircraft of ice build-up. With the TKS system, you are certified for flight into known icing, a very important feature so you're not limited in your operations.

Air Ambulance EX

As a candidate aircraft for the air ambulance role, the Grand Caravan EX is a popular choice. An air ambulance provider operating in remote environments can use a Grand Caravan EX to respond to an emergency with the aircraft quickly configured to suit the mission requirement. For example, a single life support or four-person casualty evacuation using stacked litters inside the cabin.

Model 208 Legacies

Discussing the legacies held by the Caravan and the Grand Caravan EX, Alex Hunt said: "One of the testaments to the Caravan and the Grand Caravan EX is how relevant they've

Cessna 208 Grand Caravan EX Characteristics (with cargo pod)

Length	41ft 7 in (12.7m)
Height	15ft 6 in (4.7m)
Wingspan	52ft 1 in (15.9m)
Wing Area	279ft² (25.96m²)
Wheelbase	13ft 4 in (4.05m)
Tread	11ft 8 in (3.56m)
Max ramp weight	8,842lb (4,011kg)
Max take-off weight	8,807lb (3,995kg)
Max landing weight	8,500lb (3,856kg)
Usable fuel weight	2,246lb (1,019kg)
Usable fuel volume	335 US gal (1,269lit)
Basic empty weight	5,310lb (2,409kg)
Useful load	3,532lb (1,602kg)
Max payload	3,190lb (1,447kg)
Full fuel payload	1,286lb (583kg)
Max cruise speed	185kts (343kph)
Max range	912nm (1.689km)
Take-off distance	2,160ft (658m)
Take-off ground roll	1,399ft (426m)
Landing distance	1,836ft (560m)
Max operating altitude	Up to 25,000ft (7,620m). Cabin is unpressurised so typical operations are flown between 7,000 and 10,000ft
Max climb rate	1,275ft/min (389m/pm)
Cabin height	54in (1.37m)
Cabin width	64in (1.63m)
Cabin length	21ft 4in (6.50m)
Baggage weight	1,410lb (640kg)
Baggage volume	143ft³ (4.05m³)
Max occupants	10-14
Powerplant	One Pratt & Whitney Canada PT6A-140 rated at 867shp (647kW)
Propellor	McCauley four-blade aluminium constant speed, full feathering

Source: Textron Aviation

stayed in an industry that's constantly looking at change. We haven't had to make a lot of improvements to the basic aircraft because it was well designed from the outset. Most of our engineering priorities are focused on continuing to fine tune the aircraft. The biggest changes are found in the cockpit with a lot of technology improvements, but the aircraft itself has stayed relatively the same.

"That's also a testament when defining the Caravan family of aircraft, which lies in its flexibility and reliability. These aircraft are revenue generators, so reliability is key for the operators. Many Caravan and Grand Caravan EX operators say it's one of the most reliable aeroplanes and is a defining piece of their business plan.

"In terms of flexibility, Caravan and Grand Caravan EX aircraft are just as at home on dirt, grass, or gravel strips as they are on pavement. The aircraft connect folks to the last frontiers, whether it's a traditional tribal village in Alaska where it provides access to modern medicine for them or in Indonesia to deliver supplies and disaster relief including medical evacuations. Caravan aircraft can get in and out of short strips under the most challenging conditions and are typically some of the first ones on the scene."

Cessna delivered the 2,500th Caravan aircraft in 2015, an impressive sales figure, which recently reached 3,000 in January 2023.

Through the Years

Textron Aviation provided some examples of Caravan operations based on the experiences of its customers. Starting with FedEx, the original mainline Caravan operator the other three examples give an idea of how this rugged and dependable aircraft support both people and wildlife in different parts of the world.

1985: FedEx

Baron Aviation was one of the first air freight operations to fly the Cessna Caravan on its feeder routes for FedEx. Headquartered in Vichy, Missouri, Baron operates as a Federal Express carrier throughout the south-central United States.

Back in 1985, Baron's Caravans hauled oil-field-related equipment around Texas and according to Stephen Summers, then Baron's chief pilot – caravan operations: "We haul drill bits, radioactive materials, and 'electric logs' used in drilling the wells."

Most of the time the Baron Caravans hauled from 1,500 to 2,500lb of cargo doing what can best be called flatland flying. Most of the elevations in the areas flown are between 2,500 and 3,500ft.

Though the terrain may be docile compared with mountain flying, the routes do have their tricky moments. Summers noted: "Particularly in and around Air Force Military Operating Areas. The Caravan's flexibility comes in handy when we must speed up or slow down to sequence in with the military flights. The Caravan also allows us to fly a tight traffic pattern, making steep banked turns to land when necessary."

At the time Baron Caravans fed Federal Express 727s in Austin and Lubbock, Texas and Wichita, Kansas at night, according to Summers. "Then our pilots stay over and pick up the next day's cargo there and fly back to the smaller towns. This two-flight-a-day routine continues Monday through Friday."

Baron Aviation Services has been flying Caravans for Federal Express since the Spring of 1985.

According to Summers none of Baron's pilots had any problem moving into the Caravan's single turbine, "In fact, the common reaction among our pilots has been surprise at the ease of handling and simplicity of the Caravan's turbine when compared with the piston-powered aircraft they'd been flying before."

Asked what's it like to switch from pistons to the turbine-powered Caravan? "No problem," said Summers. "The process is rapid, and our professional pilots love flying the airplane."

1997: Flying Doctors

In 1997, 53 years after first operating as a flying doctors service, AMREF of Nairobi, Kenya, found its Caravan aircraft effectively replaced three older aircraft in its fleet - older

LEFT • *A typical set of floats suitable for the Cessna Grand Caravan weigh approximately 750lb.* TEXTRON AVIATION

Cessnas, a 206, a 402, and a 404 – and cut costs.

Then owner Jim Heather Hayes said: "The Caravan's modern technology, huge cabin, long range, and flexibility all lend themselves to our company's growth. Thanks to the large payload and the number of seats, it's making the same runs we used to assign to various combinations of two older aircraft, and it does them in one flight. It'll take out a load of surgeons on Monday and another on Tuesday, then it picks them up for the return trips on Thursday and Friday. By doing two trips in one, we immediately save five hours of flying time, and that's every time we fly it. It handles the bad airstrips as well as our old 206 did, and it carries so much more. It's a very good night IFR airplane, and it's the best plane we've ever had for operating at partially lit airstrips, which we sometimes must do for medical evacuations."

In 1997, AMREF devoted 30% of the Caravan's time to making medical evacuations, 30% to taking doctors to the outlying areas on regularly scheduled flights, and the other 40% to environmental health work. Also, the Caravan sometimes undertook duty as a mobile clinic, staying on site with medical teams for up to five days at a time.

"We move engineers and construction workers around the country for many different environmental projects. And we've just supported a major rehabilitation of a hospital in Somalia. It's all part of AMREF's unique position as the only Kenyan government organisation with both long-range air transportation and trained personnel," said Hayes.

"Most of the areas we serve are remote, so the Caravan's ability to land on short, unimproved strips and to operate for lengthy periods of time without sophisticated maintenance are important attributes. It's just a fantastic, safe, and reliable bush airplane," said Hayes.

AMREF's then chief pilot Benoit Wangermez said: "The Caravan is the best medivac airplane we have. It's large, so that we can carry a doctor, a couple of nurses, and up to four patients in stretchers. We never even get close to maximum gross weight on a medivac, and it's so stable in the air that the doctors and nurses never complain about their

patients getting bounced around. But the doctors have had to resuscitate heart-attack patients in flight, and one had to do surgery on a critically ill patient in flight. They don't like to do that, but it was an emergency, and the surgery was successful."

1997: Saving Cranes and Trumpeter Swans

Since 1989, Windway Capital's chairman Terry Kohler and his wife, Mary, had been active in work to save endangered species of cranes and Trumpeter Swans. The Kohlers often personally piloted their airplanes to support these efforts, and Windway Capital's Caravan was particularly effective for carrying the birds themselves.

Kohler first became involved in his work with endangered species before he'd purchased his Caravan. In 1988, he had bought a Citation I/SP, in which he made his first deliveries of migratory species' eggs. Since then, he replaced his Citation I/SP with a Citation V, and then added a Caravan to his fleet of six aircraft. Aboard the Caravan, Windway Capital delivers live Whooping Cranes from International Crane Foundation headquarters in Baraboo and from Patuxent to the Kissimmee Prairie Wildlife Refuge in Florida.

"Live birds are more delicate than eggs, and stress can cause health problems", Kohler said. "That's why the Caravan is so important for this work. It's quiet, and that's an important consideration for these fragile animals. Also, it's fast enough and has long enough range for us to time the flight so that the birds arrive just before dark. They go into their release pen just after dark. That way, they roost and sleep for the night, and the next morning, when the sun comes up, they're gently introduced to their new surroundings."

Kohler said: "Cranes are big birds, about five feet tall, and they were cramped in the crates we had to use in the Citation. But the Caravan's cargo bay is large enough for 11 birds, each in an individual crate that gives it nearly 12 cubic feet of space. That lets them stand erect during the journey. We fit them with wing harnesses called brails, which prevent them from injuring

RIGHT • *A Grand Caravan's cargo pod extends along over two-thirds of the fuselage.* TEXTRON AVIATION

BELOW • *Operators generally use the amphibious Grand Caravan for passenger and cargo transportation to remote locations.* TEXTRON AVIATION

themselves during the trip and during the first phase of their release. Now we use the Caravan for the live birds and the Citation for the long-distance trips with eggs."

Between missions to support endangered migratory birds, Windway Capital's Caravan stays busy handling regional airline chores for Windway Capital Corporation.

Windway Capital acquired its Caravan when Kohler, a seaplane enthusiast, decided to replace his Cessna 210 and two float-equipped Cessna 206s. The Windway Caravan spends part of the year on floats and the rest on wheels.

"The floats are particularly useful when we go to Alaska to help collect Trumpeter Swan eggs," Kohler said.

He continued: "Those of us who are in the game are happy to see the Whooping Cranes recovering. The future for the Whooping Cranes is looking brighter, and we owe much of our success to George Archibald, who is the world's foremost expert on endangered species of cranes. The biggest break the cranes got was in 1989, when the US Fish and Wildlife Service decided to split its captive flock and give half of the birds to George. Close cooperation between ICF and the Patuxent Wildlife Research Center in Maryland has greatly increased captive breeding rates and release success."

1999: South African Lions

South Africa as a nation is proud of its conservation efforts. National efforts have brought back the rhinoceros from the brink of extinction. South Africa has reintroduced elephants into areas from which they had long since been chased, and it is well on its way to restoring still a third species, the lion, to areas from which it has long been absent.

Federal Air's chief executive officer Greg McCurrach said: "It surprised us when we learned our Caravans were transporting lions. Conservation Corporation Africa leased our Caravan short term, and we presumed they'd transport safari passengers as usual. But Phinda Game Preserve's veterinary surgeon needed to transport four grown lions, and the Caravan was the perfect vehicle for the job."

To avoid having one lion endure prolonged anaesthesia or captivity while vets track and dart the others, the relocation team begins darting and capturing selected individuals some weeks prior to the move. Captured lions go into a highly controlled environment called a boma, in which they have no discernible contact with humans, a requirement which keeps the animals' fear of humans high and enhances their chances of post-release survival. In the boma they develop a hierarchy of rank in the newly forming pride, and their dependency upon the pride grows.

On transfer day, crews prepare all the vehicles including the Caravan. Then the vet darts all the lions within seconds of one another. The lions go immediately onto a mat, which the crews load onto each transfer vehicle successively: then truck to the Caravan, and upon landing, they truck from the Caravan to the release site's boma. The mat prevents humans from touching the lions, thereby avoiding the lions' agitation on discovering human scent on themselves. The release site's boma is as similar as possible to the capture area's boma. There, the vets monitor the lions for a period to ensure none of the cats have suffered ill effects in the transfer. When the vets are satisfied, they release the lions into the natural environment.

Freighter by Design

Mark Ayton reviews the brand-new Cessna C408 SkyCourier

ABOVE • *SkyCourier pre-production aircraft P2 on an early test flight.* TEXTRON AVIATION

Much like the original Cessna Model 208 Caravan, the company's brand-new Model 408 SkyCourier came into being based on a FedEx Express requirement. The air delivery provider operates around 240 Caravans and Grand Caravan Cargomasters as dedicated freighters for its feeder network. According to Textron Aviation's senior technical marketing advisor, Martin Tuck, FedEx feeders now fly more than one Caravan or Cargomaster on the feeder routes. FedEx asked Textron Aviation if it could develop an aircraft with more volume, and one that would ideally allow them to transport containerised freight. This would enable the company to offload pre-sorted and pre-loaded LD2 and LD3 containers from larger aircraft and load them straight onto the new aircraft for transfer on its feeder network. Currently, FedEx must manually offload the containers, and manually load a Caravan with the up-packed freight, which is labour intensive. In those parts of the country that get very hot or cold the use of containers is very much in the forefront of their mind.

"To meet the requirement, we designed an aircraft around the capacity to carry three LD3 containers. It required a voluminous fuselage and a big door to access the cargo hold," said Tuck.

SkyCourier

The twin-engine, high-wing turboprop design was designated the Cessna Model 408 and named SkyCourier. The programme was launched on November 28, 2017, with a 50-aircraft order from FedEx Express.

Engineers working for launch customer FedEx played an integral role in defining the design parameters for the freighter version to achieve the required capabilities.

Textron Aviation formed a customer advisory board to help define the configuration of the passenger version. The OEM utilised several Caravan and Beech 1900 operators, and a couple of Twin Otter operators that provide passenger services in their respective aircraft types.

Discussing essential requirements identified by the operators, Martin Tuck said: "Firstly, they wanted to keep the large cargo door (which was surprising because we had found that most passenger aircraft had a smaller passenger-size door) and provide the ability to easily convert the cabin space to a freighter configuration by removing the seats and baggage areas. The ability to easily convert between passenger and freighter configuration increases the aircraft's revenue generating capability. The operator can provide passenger services by day and haul freight at night. This ability also keeps the aircraft's resale value up."

Two Variants

LEFT • *This shot illustrates the near-square cross-sectional profile of the SkyCourier designed to carrier LD3 containers.*
TEXTRON AVIATION

Like all OEMs, Cessna is driven by the bottom line. With its Model 408, the company offers two variants: the dedicated freighter and a 19-seat passenger version. Both variants use the same baseline airframe aside from fuselage side panels on the passenger version incorporating large windows and three emergency exits to enable carriage of passengers for airline or charter type use.

From the outset, the freighter was designed to be straightforward and robust, important factors that should make the aircraft reliable.

Discussing the PT6-65SC engine selected as the SkyCourier's powerplant, Martin Tuck said: "We use the SC designation to reflect the changes made to the engine. We added a torque limiter to provide interim protection from overzealous pilots, and sensors to the oil system. Normally you must use a ladder to climb up and visually inspect the oil level. We wanted to make the pre-flight process as easy as possible for pilots without the need for a ladder, so we fitted sensors to remotely sense the oil level and the fuel bypass filter. The oil level is shown on a multifunction display with an advisory if a top-up is required."

Aircraft features include:

- A single-point pressure refuelling port on the right-side engine nacelle.
  - LED lighting throughout the aircraft.
  - Optional air conditioning system.
  - Fixed landing gear for simplicity. No complex retractable landing gear. No hydraulic-powered extension and retraction system, purely manual controls, cables, and push rods. The landing gears are the only life-limited components on the aircraft: the nose gear life is 20,000 landings and the main gear is 28,000 landings.
  - Manual brakes.
  - Steering through the rudder pedals.
  - The all-electric aircraft uses a 28V supply.
  - A crew door on each side to avoid pilots having to use the main door.
  - A ground power hook-up point on the forward left side of the fuselage.
  - Optional weather radar.
  - Garmin G1000 NXi avionics suite with 12-inch displays, LED lighting, backlit panels, and dual USB ports for electronic flight bags.
  - Optional inflatable pneumatic boots which sequence to various sections of the wing, tail surfaces, wing struts, and the landing gear sponson for de-icing.
  - Heated glass windshields.
  - Manual flight controls.
  - Large cargo door facilitates fast and simple loading of large freight, including palletised and containerised items.
  - Optional cargo floor roller system comprising guides, rollers, and locks, which speeds up loading operations by allowing large items to be rolled fore and aft.
  - Fuselage sized for either three LD3 or four shorter LD2 containers.
  - Six floor beams run the length of the fuselage with a rated floor loading of 200lb/ft².
  - Nose baggage compartment with an 18ft3 volume and 300lb capacity.
  - A full-time engine health recorder, a trend monitoring system that records the parameters of the engine. Data is sent via WiFi for analysis to provide on-condition details and predictive maintenance.
  - Diagnostics are provided by different systems including the Garmin G1000 NXi which has its own central maintenance computer that records events and the aircraft systems recorder which runs constantly during aircraft operation, and Pratt & Whitney Canada's FAST solution which captures, analyses, and wirelessly ✈

Cessna 408 Flight-Test Aircraft

Aircraft	Registration and c/n	Test activity
Prototype	N408PR (E408-745001) made the type's first flight on May 17, 2020.	Uniquely configured for flight envelope expansion, aerodynamic, and performance testing. As required for such testing, it was fitted with a tail chute for stall testing and an emergency crew egress door in the event the aircraft became uncontrollable and the crew must bail out. Textron Aviation deployed the aircraft to Roswell, New Mexico for hot and high-performance testing. The prototype is now used for future development.
Pre-production aircraft P1	N408FR (c/n 408-0001)	Primarily engine, avionics and systems integration testing.
Pre-production aircraft P2	N408PX (c/n 408-0002)	P2 is a passenger-configured aircraft used for hot and cold weather, interior, environmental and human factor engineering testing. P2 was deployed to the McKinley Climatic Laboratory at Eglin Air Force Base, Florida to undertake hot bake and cold soak testing.

sends full-flight data intelligence to the operators base within minutes of engine shutdown. The FAST system helps to optimise maintenance planning and maximise aircraft availability.

Combi Option

Textron Aviation is also working on a combi-configured SkyCourier. As a reminder, a combi aircraft can be used to carry either passengers, or cargo as a freighter, or may have a cabin partition to allow a mixed passenger-freight combination. This configuration is suitable for essential air services which is a relatively new concept of operation in the United States. Essential air services are considered indispensable by some states and involve a subsidised service to small, remote communities that are not connected by regular airline style services. In Alaska, for example, such a service remains uneconomical for the major airlines to operate.

The Federal Aviation Administration (FAA) grants the authority to operate a scheduled air service in the form of Part 135 (Commuter) certificates. Many Part 135 operators offer critical passenger and cargo service to remote areas, providing a lifeline to populations that would not otherwise exist.

Textron Aviation has customers that operate essential services, which under regulation are limited to a nine-seat configuration. The SkyCourier aircraft is perfect for that kind of operation with nine seats in the forward hold section and freight carried in the aft. At least one Alaska-based operator has ordered aircraft in combi configuration.

By comparison, the dedicated freighter version has a forward cargo barrier to separate the pilots from the cabin while the combi version has a mid-cabin three-piece divider which enables quick installation to separate the freight from the passengers. On a combi variant, freight is loaded into the aft cargo section through the cargo door. Passengers board the aircraft through the front door into the forward cabin section.

Flight Testing and Certification

The SkyCourier prototype, registration N408PR (c/n E408-745001) made its first flight from Beech Field, Wichita on May 17, 2020. The aircraft was flown by Textron Aviation test pilots Corey Eckhart and Aaron Tobias. During the 2hrs 15mins flight the pilots tested the aircraft's performance, stability and control, the propulsion, environmental, flight control and avionics systems.

The Cessna test team used three aircraft for the SkyCourier flight-test programme and completed 2,100 hours of test time. The flight-test and certification process lasted about 22 months, FAA type-certification was awarded on March 19, 2022.

According to Martin Tuck, there weren't any real surprises discovered during the test programme. "We ended up adding some wing fences to stop span-wide flow and the hot bake testing undertaken at the McKinley Climatic Laboratory discovered the need to install a fan in the nose to cool the avionics."

During ice testing in which a SkyCourier flew behind a Citation XLS specially configured to spray water at high altitude, the water freezes onto the SkyCourier's airframe which enables the FIKI anti-icing system to be tested. Ice build-up on the sponsons led to additional ice boots being fitted. Natural icing tests were conducted in northern Canada to deliberately encounter icing and prove the FIKI system works.

Toward the end of the test programme, Textron Aviation's test team conducted functional reliability testing to prove the SkyCourier to be a fully conforming aircraft. Once that phase was complete the aircraft entered its certification period during which its racked-up 50 hours conducting all the certification requirements for the actual systems with an FAA team. The Cessna 408 SkyCourier achieved final FAA type-certification in March 2022.

Since then, Cessna has developed and certified an optional gravel kit which enables the aircraft to operate from unimproved runways. The first aircraft delivered with the gravel kit installed were made in February 2023.

Cessna delivered the first production-series aircraft, registration N408FE (c/n 408-0003) to FedEx on May 13, 2022. FedEx received FAA approval to operate the aircraft and started revenue-generating operations with Mountain Air Cargo, Florida on a run between Tallahassee and Orlando. As of February 2023, Cessna had delivered six SkyCourier aircraft to FedEx.

Production

The SkyCourier is assembled in plant four at Textron Aviation's west campus. The aircraft's tail and

LEFT • *An early shot of two SkyCourier aircraft in formation.* TEXTRON AVIATION

ABOVE · *This shot of pre-production aircraft P2 clearly shows the McCauley 110-inch heavy-duty aluminium propellors fitted with scimitar tips.* TEXTRON AVIATION

fuselage are built at a facility in Chihuahua, Mexico. The wings are built in Wichita.

Final assembly takes place on the main production line's centre aisle, one of three in plant four.

SkyCourier is assembled on a moving line comprising 14 assembly stages, each lasting 10 days. Immediately after roll-out, the aircraft goes to the paint facility and then interior finishing.

Pilot Training

Pilots destined for the SkyCourier undergo training with Flight Safety under a partnership with Textron Aviation. Pilots are type-rated based on training in a full-motion D simulator located in Wichita.

After two weeks of safety training, which includes the simulator training, a pilot gets the type rating after which they can fly a real aircraft with whatever operator they work for.

Orders

Despite a willingness to discuss orders for the SkyCourier aircraft, an FCC ruling prevents Textron Aviation from disclosing how many aircraft have been ordered or who has ordered them. The company was able to confirm that FedEx has ordered 50, though those aircraft are not the first 50, other aircraft have been ordered by an operator in Alaska and by an airline in Mexico which will receive its first aircraft in 2024. Other orders are from operators based in Hawaii (Kamaka Air) and in South America.

Cessna 408 SkyCourier Characteristics

Length	55ft 1in (16.80m)
Height	20ft 8in (6.30m)
Wingspan	72ft 2in (22.02m)
Wing Area	441ft² (40.97m²)
Wheelbase	19ft 11in (6.07m)
Tread	12ft 4in (3.76m)
Max ramp weight	19,070lb (8,650kg)
Max take-off weight	19,000lb (8,618kg)
Max landing weight	18,600lb (8,437kg)
Usable fuel weight	4,826lb (2,189kg)
Usable fuel volume	720 US gal (2,725lit)
Basic empty weight	Freighter: 11,000lb (4,990kg) Passenger: 12,325lb (5,591kg)
Basic operating weight	11,200lb (5,080kg)
Useful load	Freighter: 7,870lb (3,570kg) Passenger: 6,345lb (2,878kg)
Max payload	Freighter: 6,000lb (2,722kg) Passenger: 5,000lb (2,268kg)
Full fuel payload	Freighter: 3,044lb (1,381kg) Passenger: 1,719lb (780kg)
Max cruise speed	210kts (389km/h)
Max range	940nm (1,741km)
Take-off distance with MTOW	Freighter: 2,700ft (823m) Passenger: 3,660ft (1,115m) take-off field length
Landing distance	3,010ft (917m)
Max operating altitude	25,000ft (7,620m)
Cabin height	5ft 11in (1.80m)
Cabin width	6ft 5in (1.96m)
Cabin length	23ft 4in (7.11m)
Cargo door	7ft 3in (W) x 5ft 9in (H) 2.20m (W) x 1.75m (H)
Baggage weight passenger	1,200lb (544kg)
Cargo volume	Freighter: 884ft³ (25m³) Passenger: 186ft³ (5.27m³)
Max occupants	Freighter variant 2 Passenger variant 21
Powerplant	Two Pratt & Whitney Canada PT6A-65SC engines each rated at 1,110shp (827kW) which generates max power output in 45C temperature. The engine is suited to low-altitude high cycle operations. Overhaul interval set at 6,000 hours.
Propellor	McCauley heavy-duty C779 110-inch aluminium four-blade propeller fitted with scimitar tips, which is full feathering with reversible pitch. The propeller is optimised to enhance the performance of the aircraft. Overhaul interval set at 6,000 hours.

Source: Textron Aviation

Tarbe's Triumphant Turboprop

The TBM 700 introduced the concept of the single-engine turboprop to the business aviation community and went on to secure a leading position in that market. Continuing development of the basic airframe and systems over more than 30 years has resulted in several different variants, as David Willis recounts.

At the Paris Air Show in June 2019 Daher, Airbus and Safran unveiled plans for a distributed propulsion demonstrator based on the TBM 900-series airframe. Known as the EcoPulse project, it aims to demonstrate technology that can be incorporated in aircraft in the next decade to reduce carbon emissions. Half of the €22m funding for the programme was

provided by the French CORAC civil aviation research council.

In addition to the standard Pratt & Whitney Canada PT6A turboprop in the nose, EcoPulse has six smaller propellers on the wings, each turned by a 45kW (60hp) Safran ENGINeUS electric motor. Power for the motors is provided by a 100kW (134hp) e-APU (auxiliary power unit) mounted in the aircraft, although the inboard pair are fed by batteries. In addition to

providing thrust for the demonstrator, the outboard propellers help disperse drag-generating wingtip vortices, while the inner four contribute to lift at low speeds by blowing air over the wing.

The first flight of the EcoPulse was expected before the end of 2022, but delays caused by the COVID-19 pandemic pushed the milestone back. Although the aircraft had flown by February 2023, it had yet to do so using the distributed power system.

ABOVE • *The TBM 850, in formation with the Alpha Jet Es of the Patrouille de France. TBM 850 was the marketing name used for the first production version of the TBM 700N.* DAHERS

The EcoPulse flight test programme is expected to last 18 to 24 months.

EcoPulse is the latest – and most radical – version of the successful TBM 700 family of business aircraft. Nearly 1,100 have been delivered by the end of September 2022.

The American Connection

The roots of the TBM 700 can be traced to the Mooney M-30, a six-seat pressurised cabin design of the 1970s built to compete with the Cessna 210. At the time the American light aircraft manufacturer, based at Kerrville in Texas, lacked the resources to pursue work on the M-30 and it was not until 1980 that it was announced. By then the aircraft had become the 301 – its target speed in miles per hour – powered by a 360hp (268kW) Lycoming TIO-540-X27 flat-six piston. The prototype (N301MX) flew on April 21, 1983, with certification and deliveries expected within three years. Mooney underwent several changes of ownership in 1984 and 1985. Planned certification was initially pushed back to 1988, before the project was shelved after the company decided to instead pursue the competition for the US Air Force's new Enhanced Flight Screener. Slingsby eventually emerged with that contract with a version of the T67M Firefly.

By 1985 the majority of Mooney (70%) was owned by Alexandre Couvelaire, with the other 30% held by Armand Rivard of Lake Aircraft, with the financial backing of French investor Michel Seydoux. Couvelaire had been a dealer for Mooney Aircraft in Paris. Around the same time SOCATA (Société de Construction d'Avions de Tourisme et d'Affaires), a division of Aérospatiale, was looking to progress beyond its family of piston-engined TB four-seat tourers (TB standing for Tarbes, the French city it was based at). It wanted a new design with high-speed and altitude capabilities to which existing TB customers could progress. At some point it was realised that the Mooney 301 was a useful starting point, although it would have to be redesigned with a turboprop to meet the speed and altitude requirements. While the TBM 700 that eventually emerged was radically different from the Mooney 301, it served to bring the two companies together. They would go on to form TBM International, 70% owned by SOCATA and 30% by Mooney (the 'M' in TBM).

LEFT • *The TBM 900 is an extensive overhaul of the TBM 850 with significantly improved performance. External changes were few, the most obvious is the addition of winglets.* DAHER

BELOW LEFT • *The first and second TBM 700 prototypes (registrations F-WTBM and second F-WKPG) in flight during the second half of 1999. F-WKPG was converted as the first TBM 850 and made the type's first flight in February 2005.* AIRBUS

Development

The project was officially launched on June 12, 1987. SOCATA would be responsible for technical development and certification, plus manufacture of the forward fuselage and empennage. Mooney would construct the wings and rear fuselage and establish a US production line for the aircraft.

The need for a reliable powerplant for the TBM 700 resulted in the selection of the Pratt & Whitney Canada PT6, which had first flown in May 1961 and had been the subject of continuous development ever since. Among the aircraft it powered was the Beech King Air series, one of the types TBM hoped to replace with its design, and was a known, dependable item. Well over 50,000 have been produced and by

October 2003 it had recorded only one in-flight shutdown for every third of a million hours of operation.

Three prototype TBM 700s were built by SOCATA. The first (F-WTBM) completed its maiden flight on July 14, 1988, and was followed by the other pair on August 3 and October 11, 1989. The flight test programme proceeded smoothly, resulting in the TBM 700 receiving its Type Certificate from the French authorities on January 31, 1990, followed by the US Federal Aviation Administration (FAA) on August 28.

The TBM 700 was the first commercial single-engine turboprop to enter production. Deliveries commenced on December 21, 1990, and 71 had been ordered by April the next year. The aircraft appealed to both owner-operators and corporations alike, its performance and lower operating costs in comparison to twin-turboprops then on the market helping to swell the order book. Early operators also praised its speed and power at altitude.

The initial success resulted in SOCATA having to invest heavily to improve the worldwide support infrastructure for the aircraft, which was initially judged to be poor by operators. This changed as the 1990s progressed as new service centres were opened, helping pave the way for greater penetration of the American market. The United States would go on to become the largest market for the TBM 700 and the family it spawned.

This should have been good news for Mooney, but it was not able to benefit from the popularity of the TBM 700. In May 1991 Mooney announced it was leaving the TBM International partnership. The 1980s had been a torrid time for US general aviation manufacturers, and by the early 1990s Mooney was suffering financial difficulties and could not afford to establish a US line for the TBM 700. Instead, it decided to concentrate on its M20 series.

French Military Service

An early adopter of the TBM 700 was the Armée de l'air (French Air Force), which acquired a total of 20, including some for the Centre d'Essais en Vol (CEV). Deliveries began on May 27, 1992, when the first of an initial six was handed over, going to the Groupe Aérien d'Entrainement et de Liaison (GAEL) and Escadron de Transport & d'Entraînement (ETE) 43 'Médoc'. A second order for another six was fulfilled in 1993-4 and additional orders followed.

The Aviation légère de l'Armée de terre (ALAT, French Army Light Aviation) received its first pair on January 13, 1995, for 3 Groupe d'Helicopteres Legers at Rennes-Saint-Jacques-de-la-Lande. A further six were delivered, three of which were TBM 700Bs, a variant optimised to carry freight with a large cargo door, the last of which was handed over to the ALAT on June 28, 2000. The fleet was augmented by four former air force examples in 2006, one of which was later returned. In early 2023 nine remained active with the EAAT (l'escadrille Avions de l'armée de terre), while a former army TBM 700A is operated by the Direction Générale de l'Armement Essais en Vol (DGA-EV, as the CEV became in 2009). The retitled Armée de l'air et de l'espace currently has 16 TBM 700As in its inventory.

France remains the only nation to have put the TBM 700 family into military service. While its TBM 700s are used as light transports, a surveillance variant was developed as the TBM MMA (Multi-Mission Aircraft) equipped with a sensor turret (of the customer's choice) under the rear fuselage and operator's console in the cabin. The first example was delivered

ABOVE LEFT • *TBM 700 N715MC was the 30th production aircraft built which rolled out in 1991. The initial version of the aircraft became the TBM 700A after the introduction of a light freight variant, the TBM 700B.* AIRBUS

LEFT • *The TBM MMA (Multi-Mission Aircraft) is a special missions' version of the family, equipped with a retractable sensor turret under the rear fuselage. This demonstrator was based on the TBM 850.* DAHER

ABOVE • *The TBM 930 was the second of the 900-series developed, with a Garmin G3000 avionics suite in place of the Garmin G1000 avionics fitted in the TBM 900. Daher has continued to offer variants of the aircraft with either touchscreen or keypad operated avionics.* DAHER

RIGHT • *TBM 850 N426TB was built in 2012, the year that a quick-change variant was introduced as the 850 Elite.* DAHER

to Argentina's Airport Security Police in 2011. More than 40 TBM MMAs equipped for intelligence surveillance and reconnaissance, medical evacuation or navaid calibration have been delivered based on the TBM 700 and subsequent models.

TBM 700C

With the formation of the European Aeronautic, Defence and Space Company (EADS) on July 10, 2000, from the assets of Aerospatiale Matra of France and DASA (DaimlerChrysler Aerospace) of Germany, SOCATA became a 100% owned subsidiary of the new organisation. It continued to improve the TBM 700, flying the first prototype TBM 700C1 in February 2002, which was followed by the higher-weight C2 variant. The two 'C' versions had a strengthened spar box and wing attachments, and better air conditioning. An additional unpressurised baggage compartment was created at the rear of the cabin, while the interior furnishings were refreshed. The TBM 700C2 also had new wheels to cope with the additional weight and cabin seats able to withstand 20g.

The TBM 700C became the standard production version from 2002, with certification of the C2 by the FAA on March 7, 2003, and by EASA on July 14, 2004. The TBM 700C2 was the last variant marketed as the 700-series. In

all, 324 TBM 700s were produced.

Improving the Breed

In August 2004, EADS SOCATA launched the TBM 850 programme, the first major overhaul of the design. Like the TBM 700 before it, the designation TBM 850 derived from the horsepower of its turboprop. While the TBM 700 had a Pratt & Whitney Canada PT6A-64 flat rated to 700shp (522kW), the TBM 850 was equipped with a PT6A-66D that retained that limit for take-off but could boost power to 850shp (634kW) in the cruise, providing a corresponding increase in performance. Maximum cruise speed rose by 20kts (37km/h)

to 320kts (592km/h) at 26,000 ft (7,925m), and range from 1,350nm (2,500km) to 1,580nm (2,778km). The second prototype TBM 700 (F-WKPG) was converted as the first TBM 850 and flew again in February 2005. EADS SOCATA publicly announced the aircraft in December 2005, after EASA certification (as the TBM 700N) had been received on November 28. The initial production TBM 850 flew on January 23, 2006.

The '2008 model' TBM 850 introduced Garmin G1000 avionics to the family, replacing the Bendix/King Silver Crown system of the earlier aircraft. Additional changes introduced included improvements to the air conditioning, a redesigned interior with greater space, reduced airframe weight, and a slightly higher fuel capacity with range increasing to 1,409nm (2,609km) at cruise speed. The first G1000-equipped TBM 850 was delivered on January 24, 2008, to the owner of Big Bike Parts of Wisconsin. A total of 338 members of the TBM 850 family had been delivered by the time production ended.

Change of Ownership

While SOCATA was profitable, it accounted for less than 1% of EADS' total turnover. In June 2008 the company announced it was selling a 70% stake in it to the French industrial concern Daher, the deal being completed on November 3, 2008. Its new division became Daher-SOCATA. The sale occurred just as the banking crisis began to bite, resulting in nearly half of the deliveries planned for 2009 being deferred. The previous year SOCATA had handed over a record 60 TBM 850s, of which most went to American customers and 20% went to European.

Daher introduced the TBM 850 Elite in 2012. It featured a quick-change capability for the cabin, which allowed the rearmost pair of the six seats in the cabin to be removed so that more luggage could be accommodated. Changes in the cockpit included the option of a long-range radio

and transceiver, providing non-US customers with meteorological information and near real-time positioning.

In January 2013 the worldwide TBM fleet passed its one millionth hour in the air. Later the same year glass cockpit upgrades were announced for the TBM 700/850, based on Garmin G600 avionics, which replaced the first generation EFIS displays in the aircraft. The first modified TBM 700 was redelivered in January 2014.

The Airbus Group (as EADS had become) sold its remaining 30% interest to Daher in June 2014 and early the next year the SOCATA name was discontinued. Full control of the TBM programme allowed Daher to implement plans to continuously upgrade the aircraft to incorporate the latest avionics with additional functionality and refresh the cabin to conform to changing tastes and compatibility with the latest hand-held electrical devices, as well as refine the airframe. Subsequent members of the Daher TBM family are all technically versions of the TBM 700N (marketed as the TBM 850) with different modification packages developed by the company.

Small Changes, Big Improvements

Even before it took full control of the programme, Daher had begun to investigate a second generation

of the basic TBM 700 design. The aim was to produce an aircraft with better performance and handling that was quieter and had a lower carbon footprint. The key to enhancing the aircraft was to refine its aerodynamics, while making use of the latest computer-aided design techniques which hadn't been available when the TBM was originally conceived, and composite materials. A five (rather than four) blade propeller was selected, while the efficiency of the intake and cooling for the PT6A-66D turboprop was improved. The addition of winglets allowed all 850shp (634kW) to be used with the flaps down – unlike in the TBM 850 – permitting full power from take-off throughout the flight, as well as improving handling, climb and cruise performance.

A new tail cone was added, increasing length by 10cm (4in), while the main wheel doors were cleaned up. Many of the aircraft's systems were improved, such as the addition of automatic pressurisation for the cabin, an auto-start for the PT6 and a torque limiter, while more electrical power was provided by a higher rated generator. New controls were added to the yokes in the cockpit, while larger pilots benefited from the additional knee room created by redesigning the instrument panel. While the Garmin G1000 avionics were retained, new software made it more user friendly. In total 26 modifications were made to

LEFT • *CThe TBM 910 is the third member of the 900-series and fitted with the latest version of the Garmin G1000 avionics suite. The TBM 910 remains one of two variants still in production.* DAVID WILLIS

RIGHT • *Garmin G3000-equipped TBM 940 F-GCKJ was built in 2019 and later sold in the United States. The TBM 940 was recently replaced on the production line by the TBM 960, powered by a new version of the trusty PT6 turboprop.* DAVID WILLIS

Daher TBM 910 Characteristics

Wingspan	12.83m (42ft 1in)
Length	10.74m (35ft 2in)
Height	4.35m (14ft 3in)
Max take-off weight	3,354kg (7,394lb)
Max landing weight	3,186kg (7,023lb)
Max zero fuel weight	2,736kg (6,031lb)
Operating empty weight	2,097kg (4,623lb)
Useable fuel	291 US gal (1,106 lit)
Max cruise speed at 28,000ft	330kts (611km/h) max cruising speed at FL280
Ceiling	31,000ft (9,450m) max operating altitude
Seating	Eight typical, including one or two pilot(s)
Range	1,584nm (2,933km) at normal cruise with 45 min reserves
Engine	One Pratt & Whitney Canada PT6A-66D flat-rated to 850shp (634kW)

the TBM 850. The result was the TBM 900.

Daher flight tested many of the new features on a modified TBM 700 from late 2010. That aircraft was later joined by a pair of new build examples, with the trio conducting a 215-hour flight test campaign leading to the update of the EASA Type Certificate to include the TBM 900 on December 2, 2013, and the FAA equivalent in the same month. The TBM 900 raised cruising speed to 330kts (611km/h) at 28,000ft (8,534m), and increased range by over 300nm (560km), primarily thanks to measures made to reduce fuel burn and improve the aerodynamics. Daher announced the new version in March 2014 and initial deliveries to three customers in the United States and Europe occurred later that month. By then Daher held 40 orders for the aircraft.

TBM 900-Series
Daher had built only 114 TBM 900s by the time production of the model ended in 2016. The relatively small number of TBM 900s produced was down to the decision by the company to market upgrades of the aircraft with different designations. This would eventually result in the TBM 930, 910, 940, and 960 which introduced a range of new systems and capabilities.

The TBM 930 was certified on February 18, 2016, and unveiled on April 5 to selected guests at Tarbes, making its public debut two days later at Sun 'n' Fun at Lakeland, Florida. The variant was a TBM 900 with Garmin G3000 touchscreen avionics plus a Mid-Continent Instruments MD302 standby altitude module, and an interior with redesigned seating. Rheinland Air Service of Germany accepted the first on April 20, 2016, and five had been delivered by the end of the month. The variant remained

available until it was replaced by the TBM 940 in 2019, which added autothrottles as standard, increased automation for the de-icing system and had a new cabin interior with better thermal insulation.

In mid-2020 the TBM 940 HomeSafe system was introduced as an option for new and existing aircraft. An emergency landing system based on the Garmin Autoland, it can be activated manually or automatically to land the aircraft should the pilot become incapacitated. Autoland is integrated with the G3000 avionics and once selected picks the best airfield to land at, considering available fuel and runway length. Air traffic control is alerted, the aircraft's transponder code is set to the emergency quark code, and the aircraft is flown to touchdown. Upon landing the brakes are applied and the engine shut down at the end of the roll. Daher began integrating the system in the TBM in 2017 and had completed over 200 automatic landings before it was approved by both the US and European aviation authorities.

Daher announced the TBM 910 in April 2017 as a direct replacement for the baseline TBM 900. The most significant change was the replacement of the G1000 suite with the G1000NXi, which has greater processing power and brighter, clearer displays, while the cabin was refreshed to match that of the TBM 930. It was certified in Europe and the United States in late March 2017 and deliveries began the following month.

The fifth evolution and, as of early 2023, latest of the 900-series is the TBM 960, which replaced the 940 in Daher's range and retains the earlier model's G3000 avionics. Its most significant change is the introduction to the TBM family of the PT6E-66XT turboprop, rated at 895shp (667kW),

with a dual-channel digital engine and propeller electronic control system, turning a five-blade Hartzell Raptor propeller. The TBM 960 also comes equipped with the latest Garmin GWX8000 weather radar and benefits from a 221lb (100kg) increase in maximum take-off weight, to 7,615lb (3,454kg). Daher handed over the first TBM 960 to a German businessman in April 2022, after EASA approval the previous month.

The TBM 960 remains the current touchscreen avionics production variant of the 900-series and is offered alongside the TBM 910 fitted with the push-button G1000NXi. In recent years G3000-equipped variants have greatly outsold those with the G1000NXi – 78 to two in the 21 months from the start of 2021. This may help shape the direction of Daher's plan for the TBM family.

Twin Otter

Malcolm Ginsberg details the resurrection of the DHC-6 Twin Otter 400 Series under Viking Air's ownership.

ABOVE • VIKING AIR

In a momentous announcement at the Farnborough International Airshow on July 17, 2006, Viking Air Ltd unveiled its intention to offer a new version of the de Havilland Canada DHC-6 Twin Otter two-engine 19-passenger turboprop. Although many designs have experienced production breaks for all sorts of reasons, the last Twin Otter had been built in 1988.

Since acquiring the rights to the design, Viking Air sales support staff and senior executives visited current and prospective operators around the world to gauge interest in either an entirely new utility aircraft, possibly with a pressurised cabin, or a complete update of the Twin Otter Series 300 that last left the line in 1988. Viking Air

soon confirmed that the latter option, christened the Twin Otter Series 400, held the greatest appeal.

By April 2007, Viking Air was able to confirm that, with 27 orders and options in hand, it would restart assembly of the Twin Otter, equipped with the latest and more powerful Pratt & Whitney Canada PT6A-34 engine.

Legacy Designs

Viking Air was established in 1970 by Norwegian-born Canadian aviation pioneer, Nils Christensen, essentially as an overhaul and maintenance organisation specialising in Grumman flying boats and de Havilland Canada float planes. In 1983, Christensen acquired from de Havilland Canada the exclusive rights to manufacture spare parts for the DHC-2 Beaver

and DHC-3 Otter. In May 2005, the company purchased the parts and service business for all legacy de Havilland Canada aircraft from Bombardier Aerospace. A year later, Bombardier sold it the type certificates for all out-of-production de Havilland Canada designs: the DHC-1 Chipmunk, DHC-2 Beaver, DHC-3 Otter, DHC-4 Caribou, DHC-5 Buffalo, DHC-6 Twin Otter and DHC-7 Dash 7. It conferred on Viking Air the right to manufacture and sell new-built examples of the aircraft. The ongoing Bombardier Dash 8 programme and de Havilland Canada brand was also acquired in November 2018 by Viking Air's parent company, Longview Aviation Capital, which continues to produce the Q400 turboprop airliner.

The resurrection of the Twin Otter

came as no surprise to industry observers. The prototype made its maiden flight on May 25, 1965, and over 23 years 844 examples were built at the Downsview facility in Toronto, Ontario, home of de Havilland Canada since 1928. Around 470 were still active and the type was much in demand in the pre-used market as few alternative types in its category were available.

New Generation

The first flight of the Series 400 technical demonstrator – a modified Series 300 – occurred on October 1, 2008, at Victoria International Airport in British Columbia, Canada. The aircraft was configured as a multi-function development machine fitted with Wipline 13000 amphibious floats.

Core cockpit avionics comprised a Honeywell Primus Apex digital suite, with two primary flight displays and two multifunction displays with clear, high-resolution active-matrix liquid crystal displays and wide viewing capability, allowing for cross-cockpit scanning. Apex integrates aircraft systems, safety sensors and navigation information, reducing cockpit workload and improving safety by enhancing the pilots' situational awareness.

The digital flight deck and uprated engines were the major changes from the earlier versions of the aircraft. Less visible was the reduction in empty weight, achieved by making use of composites for non-loadbearing structures, including the doors, nosecone, and fairings.

Production

On February 16, 2020, Viking Air celebrated the tenth anniversary of the inaugural flight of the first new-built Series 400. This first aircraft, manufacturer's serial number (MSN) 845, made its maiden flight from the company's final aircraft assembly facility in Calgary, Alberta. Since delivery as HB-LUX to Zimex, a Swiss specialist charter airline, it has been used to provide essential humanitarian relief and corporate charter services in Africa and the Middle East.

The second Viking-produced Twin Otter, MSN 846, was delivered to Air Seychelles, which uses the aircraft to carry passengers from its base in Mahé to outlying islands of the Seychelles archipelago in the Indian Ocean.

The first float-equipped aircraft, MSN 848, was delivered to Trans Maldivian Airways (TMA), working in conjunction with more than 40 legacy

LEFT • *Fitted with floats, Viking Air demonstrator DHC-6-400 C-FDHT (msn 434) takes off from a lake* VIKING AIR

Twin Otters in operation in the region. TMA's second aircraft (MSN 849) joined a fleet of 23 legacy Twin Otters operating out of the unique seaplane terminal at Male International Airport. It is a short walk from the 'real' airport to the busy floatplane terminal.

One niche in which the Twin Otter has proven popular is that of skydiving. In November 2015, Skydive Dubai purchased three Series 400 aircraft to join its fleet of legacy Twin Otters.

Further Upgrades

By September 2015, Viking Air had launched the Series 400 Phase II avionics upgrade package, significantly increasing functionality of the Primus Apex system in the aircraft. It included a three-axis autopilot, Traffic Collision Avoidance System II, an FAA-compatible engine instrument display, a wide area augmentation system, coupled vertical navigation, localiser performance with vertical guidance, Automatic Dependent Surveillance-Broadcast Out (ADS-B Out), the SmartView synthetic vision system, and a flight data recorder.

The Farnborough International Airshow has always proved a popular meeting place for Viking Air and its customers from around the world. At the 2016 event, the company disclosed that the 100th production Series 400, MSN 944, had flown. It was delivered to Pacific Sky Aviation Inc, a company belonging to Viking Air's parent.

With the delivery of the 100th aircraft, the variant was in service with 34 different customers operating in 38 countries.

In 2019, Air Antilles became the first commercial operator to receive European Union Aviation Safety Agency (EASA) approval for steep landings in the Series 400, allowing the airline to

operate at approach angles more than 4.5°. This was essential for Air Antilles' scheduled operations at Gustaf III Airport in Saint Barthélemy, a French colony in the Caribbean. EASA requires all commercial aircraft operating from the site to have factory certification for steep approach landings due to the mountainous terrain surrounding the airport.

At the end of 2019, the Avmax Group of Calgary, Alberta, took delivery of two new Series 400s configured for corporate shuttle operations in support of oil and gas operations in the Republic of Chad.

Argentina's Federal Police placed an order for a single Series 400 aircraft, pilot training in Canada and flight simulation for six Argentinean pilots in December 2019. The second phase of the deal involved equipping the aircraft for firefighting and installation with other enhanced systems.

Prior to the Argentinian order, Viking Air had announced the certification by Transport Canada of the first Twin Otter Full Flight Simulator through its sister company Pacific Sky Aviation. The Series 400 simulator replicates the aircraft's cockpit, avionics systems and flight behaviour, giving instructors the ability to programme training events from any airport or GPS location, a valuable feature for customers operating from remote regions or conducting special operations. It also offers seaplane pilots the opportunity to safely practice take-offs and landings in a range of sea states, winds, and water conditions, including glassy water.

Military Configurations

In response to enquiries from foreign military and government

DHC-6-400 Characteristics

Wingspan	19.8m (65ft)
Length	15.77m (51ft 9in)
Tail height	5.94m (19ft 6in)
Max take-off weight	5,670kg (12,500lb)
Max landing weight	5,579kg (12,300lb)
Operating empty weight	3,377kg (7,445lb)
Useable fuel	291 US gal (1,436 lit)
Max cruise speed at 10,000ft	182kts (337km/h)
Max operating altitude	25,000ft (7,620m)
Cabin length	18ft 5in (5.61m)
Cabin height	4ft 11in (1.5m)
Cabin width	5ft 9in (1.75m)
Cabin volume	384ft^3 (10.87m^3)
Main cabin entry	50 x 56in (1.27 x 1.42m)
Seating	Standard layout is a 19-seat configuration, excluding one or two pilot(s)
Payload range for 400nm	1,375kg (3,031lb)
Engine	Two Pratt & Whitney Canada PT6A-34 single stage, free turbine engines each rated at 750shp (559kW)

Source: Viking Air

agencies, Viking Air released preliminary data about the Guardian 400 at the Paris Air Show in June 2009. The Series 400 variant was offered for medium range maritime patrol, search and rescue (SAR), critical infrastructure surveillance and security operations. It was promoted as a cost-effective solution with low acquisition and operating costs, equipped with a modern, flexible sensor package tailored to the customer's operational requirements. Guardian 400s account for 25% of production.

The Guardian 400 includes a restricted category increased take-off weight and extended range internal patrol tank, allowing for operational sorties of more than ten hours' duration. It can be outfitted with an electro-optical and infrared imaging turret, images from which can be displayed on either the digital Primus Apex flight deck or a console in the cabin. Other features offered include a spotter camera, laser range finder and a laser illuminator. Additionally, the aircraft can be fitted with a lightweight 360° digital colour radar system with track-while-scan capability, including long-range navigation position update, target position transmission, location latitude and longitude, target heading and velocity. Configured for SAR and maritime patrol roles, the Guardian 400 can be equipped with four crew observation stations, a rescue equipment drop hatch, an air operable cargo door, searchlight, galley, and toilet. As with the civilian Series 400, float, ski, or wheel landing gear (including the intermediate flotation gear large tyres option for a soft field

capability) are offered, while four wing hard points can be mounted for external stores.

Twin Otter Seaplane

After decades of Twin Otter floatplane operations with legacy and Series 400 aircraft, Viking Air launched the latest version, the Twin Otter 400S Seaplane, at the 2016 Singapore Airshow. Series 400 customers can pick a straight floatplane conversion, which involves the installation of Wipline 13000SEA floats (together with float reinforcements, flight control cables and propellers with prop pitch latches). The Wipline floats can also be provided as a standalone item for operators wanting to switch between floats and standard landing gear, and there is an option to install amphibious Wipline floats.

The Twin Otter 400S is fitted with PT6A-27 engines as standard, versus the PT6A-34 fitted on the Series 400, features the Honeywell Super-Lite integrated digital avionics suite adapted for visual flight rules and instrument flight rules operations, and new-generation composite floats as standard. The 400S can carry up to 19 passengers or 15 passengers and some cargo in a combi configuration.

Commercial Operations

Viking Air says it specifically developed the 400S, "to optimise the Twin Otter platform for commercial seaplane operations" on short to medium flights. To help maximise appeal to companies operating in this market, the company has designed the 400S for quick turnarounds. It says the aircraft, "can

LEFT •*Two Viking Air DHC-6-400 aircraft. In the foreground, C-FDHT (msn 434) was originaly built in 1974 as a DHC-6-300. This aircraft crashed in the Maldives in 2004 and was rebuilt as a DHC-6-400 Series developmental engineering prototype, which first flew on October 1, 2008. C-FUVA (msn 851) was built as a 400 Series in 2011 and fitted with floats for use as a demonstrator aircraft.* VIKING AIR

ABOVE • *DHC-6-400 C-GVKI (msn 897) was built in 2014 as a Series 400 Guardian. The aircraft is seen in a Viking Air demonstrator paint scheme.* VIKING AIR

achieve a breakeven load factor of around eight passengers under typical operating conditions."

A Viking Air spokeswoman told the author: "During the development stage, we interviewed existing seaplane operators worldwide to understand what worked [and what didn't work] for them, and where possible, we've incorporated their suggestions into the 400S baseline. For example, the 400S seaplane features a second avionics-dedicated battery to keep the screens live during turnover."

The aircraft will also have modified double swing-out aft passenger doors and internal access to the rear baggage area through the aft cabin to further increase the efficiency of loading and unloading passengers and cargo. The spokeswoman said: "While there has been no change to the type certificate, our engineering team has made a series of minor modifications to incorporate the desired changes within the type design."

Maintenance and Corrosion Resistance

Viking Air wanted to reduce maintenance costs and downtime for operators with the 400S, so what savings can operators expect?

A company spokesperson replied: "The PT6A-27 engine is renowned as an absolute workhorse for water-based operations, and when combined with the composite floats, lower line replaceable unit count in the avionics design and additional corrosion protection, there is an expectation that downtime due to maintenance issues will be significantly reduced. The standard equipment and modifications on the 400S have all been selected to optimise the aircraft for operation in the harshest of conditions."

Using carbon fibre composites for the floats instead of the metal used on previous Twin Otter seaplane configurations is designed to ease maintenance, provide weight savings, and improve resistance to the corrosion associated with operating in saline environments.

Corrosion was one of the operational aspects Viking Air specifically asked seaplane operators about when it held discussions about maintenance issues with customers during the 400S development process. Besides the composite floats, the manufacturer decided to address those needs by incorporating several packages into the 400S design to minimise corrosion. These are:

- Engine Water Operation Package: This includes (but is not limited to) platinum-coated CT blades, stainless-steel engine control cables and the removal of the intake deflector.

- Fuel System Water Operation Package: This includes (but is not limited to) additional water drain valves, a fuel control unit purge valve, additional fuel galley sealing, an upgrade to the boost pump and the installation of corrosion resistant fuel line coating.

- Airframe Water Operation Package: This includes (but is not limited to) the application of corrosion prevention primer, an upgraded hydraulic bay door and the installation of stainless-steel flight control cables.

Orders Outlook

When Viking Air announced the 400S at the Farnborough International Airshow in July 2006, the company forecast: "increasing sales potential" and estimated a potential market for seaplanes as large as 100-plus aircraft.

Were there prospects for the 400S in terms of existing seaplane operators looking for more seating and/or newer equipment? "Absolutely," a company spokeswoman replied. "There are several Series 300 Twin Otters still flying that are 30-plus years old, and the 400S is the ideal replacement candidate. With the base price set under $6 million including full warranty package, the 400S is the perfect alternative to spending money on upgrading a legacy Twin Otter float plane. In addition, the 400S is a natural progression for Caravan or Kodiak operators looking to step up to a twin engine aircraft."

Ocean Observer

Jon Lake reviews the de Havilland Canada DHC-8 maritime surveillance aircraft.

The Elta maritime search radar, and Swedish Space Corporation SLAR, fitted to a Swedish Coast Guard DHC-8-300.
FIELD AVIATION

In today's cost-conscious times many maritime surveillance tasks traditionally performed by expensive, dedicated military anti-submarine warfare aircraft are increasingly being undertaken by civil based platforms that provide superior availability and that can achieve the task at a fraction of the cost. Of these cheaper, airliner-based Maritime Surveillance Aircraft (MSA), the de Havilland Canada DHC-8 (dubbed the Dash 8) has been proven to be the machine of choice.

DHC-8 Evolution

Though designed and best known as a rugged, turboprop-powered airliner, with some of the formidable short take-off and landing capabilities that one would expect from de Havilland Canada, the DHC-8 was a natural choice for conversion for special missions use, with its modest fuel consumption endowing it with a respectable mission radius, and with its short take-off and landing

(STOL) capabilities allowing operation from a wide range of airfields. Against these advantages, the slightly lower cruising speed (compared to regional jets) is of little importance.

The original DHC-8 led the new generation of twin turboprop airliners that entered service during the 1980s. This soon became a crowded field. The baseline 37-39 seat DHC-8-100 was followed by a stretched DHC-8-300 with increased power, an 11ft (3.35m) fuselage plug and with accommodation for 50-56 passengers. The short DHC-8-200 model combined the original airframe with the 300's more powerful engine. The later DHC-8-400 introduced an even more dramatic stretch and seated 70-78 passengers.

From Q2 1996 all DHC-8s delivered (including all Series 400s) were fitted with a passive and later an Active Noise and Vibration Suppression (ANVS) system. This was designed to reduce cabin noise and vibration levels to something approaching those experienced in the cabins of

ABOVE • *Australian Coastwatch DHC-8 VH-ZZJ on patrol with a merchant ship in the background.*
FIELD AVIATION

RIGHT • *DHC-8 VH-ZZB taxiing at Truscott Air Base, in the far north of Western Australia.*
MARTIN EADIE

ABOVE • *The under-fuselage configuration of the E-9A aircraft which features a black radome and a white canoe, housing the antennas for the APS-143(V)1 Airborne Sea Surveillance Radar.*
US AIR FORCE

contemporary jet airliners. Bombardier, the then owner of the types, re-named its DHC-8-200, DHC-8-300, and DHC-8-400 models as the Q200, Q300 and Q400.

It is perhaps appropriate that the principal companies involved in turning this iconic Canadian airliner into an iconic maritime patroller are both themselves Canadian.

Modifiers

Field Aviation, based in Toronto, Ontario and Calgary, Alberta, is a leading provider of aircraft modifications and related services (including sales, parts manufacturing, and technical services) to a range of commercial, government and military customers worldwide, and has become a recognised market leader in modifying heavy turboprop and turbofan commercial aircraft for special mission roles, as well as for providing end-to-end solutions requiring cost-efficient, reliable airborne platforms.

The company has become the leading modifier of DHC-8s for the maritime surveillance role and other special mission applications.

Field's customers include Surveillance Australia (now Cobham Aviation Services Australia), who operate ten DHC-8-400 MSAs. Field has also completed delivery of three DHC-8 Series 300 MSAs to the Kustbevakning (Swedish Coast Guard) registrations SE-MAA (msn 622), SE-MAB (msn 631), and SE-MAC (msn 638), and a single Series 300 TF-SIF (msn 660) delivered to the Landhelgisgæslan (Icelandic Coast Guard).

Between 2003 to 2009, Field Aviation modified and delivered seven DHC-8 MSAs to the US Customs and Border Protection service, four based on the Series 200 aircraft and three on the larger Series 300.

The CBP programme emphasised commonality and interchangeability between the Series 200 and Series 300 aircraft.

Field Aviation said: "This objective was achieved by designing all elements of the DHC-8 MSA modification to maximise common use, regarding the structural changes and the provisions and components introduced. Examples of common parts across all DHC-8 MSAs that have been modified by Field Aerospace include common radome with jig-drilled mounting provisions that fit all search radars installed; common installation for Wescam MX-15 and Teledyne FLIR Star Safire multi-spectral turrets; common observation windows/ type III emergency exits; common operator and observer seats and seat adapters; and common upgrades to APU electrical power."

According to Field: "The CBP was the first MSA customer to take advantage of Field Aviation's STC to increase

LEFT • *Resplendent in its overall blue paint scheme, CT-142 142803 is one of four assigned to the Royal Canadian Air Force's 402 Squadron.*
ROYAL CANADIAN AIR FORCE

based Provincial Aerospace Limited (PAL Aerospace) has less experience in DHC-8 MSA conversions than Field but did win a United Arab Emirates' hard-fought competition for a new maritime patrol aircraft.

PAL Aerospace has extensive special mission modification and integration experience on a variety of aircraft platforms. It operates a fleet of five DHC-8 series maritime patrol aircraft under contract to government and military clients worldwide.

The company offers clients a programme designed to deliver self-sufficient, mission-ready aircraft for complex maritime surveillance anywhere in the world known as Force Multiplier. PAL Aerospace says: "Aircraft

are available with a complete crew complement and integral maintenance capability on an hourly, monthly or long-term leased basis, alleviating the costs and logistical burdens of adopting surveillance and reconnaissance capability for any length of time."

Variants

The DHC-8 MSA aircraft delivered to different customers differ in detail, but most share some common features. Most are based on the quieter ANVS-equipped aircraft, which provides a superior working environment for the crews, and about half are based on the stretched DHC8-300.

Though the aircraft usually carry relatively small crews, the bigger

ABOVE • The Swedish Coast Guard (Kustbevakning) operates three DHC-8-300 aircraft, which are fitted with Field's air operable door. This shot shows an aircraft deploying an inflatable life raft via the opening. FIELD AVIATION

RIGHT • Swedish Coast Guard DHC-8-300 CG 502. FIELD AVIATION

BELOW • In December 2006 the Japan Coast Guard selected the DHC-8-300 MSA for maritime patrol and search and rescue duties within the nation's area of maritime responsibility. JASON PINEAU

the maximum take-off weight for the DHC-8-200 MSA from 36,300lb to 37,300lb. The STC adds a 1,000lb payload capacity or extends the mission endurance by one hour with the same payload - without having any impact on the aircraft's structural life or frequency of structural inspections."

The Japan Coast Guard ordered nine DHC-8-300 MSAs, which were delivered between January 2009 and February 2014.

Field Aviation also undertook the partial modification of three DHC-8s for an undisclosed customer for use in the special mission role, and these were delivered in 2007.

The company has also modified a DHC-8-300 for the Japan Civil Aviation Bureau for flight inspection.

With just two aircraft in service (company-owned DHC-8s used to fulfil a Netherlands Antilles and Aruba Coast Guard contract) and two more on order, the St John's, Newfoundland-

DHC8-300 allows the carriage of more relief crew members, or ground crew and support personnel for deployed operations, while the larger cabin also gives more space for mission equipment and/or auxiliary fuel tanks. The DHC-8-200 and DHC-8-300 based MSAs are equipped with long-range fuel tanks in the wings (giving more than eight hours endurance), and the DHC-8-300s also have provision for additional cabin fuel. The aircraft have an auxiliary power unit to provide autonomy from ground support equipment when operating from forward operating bases. Based on available data, compared to older turboprop types, the DHC-8-300 MSA offers significantly higher mission availability and much lower operating costs, and the aircraft's speed shortens transit times, and gives more time on station.

With the same fuel load in a smaller, lighter aircraft, the DHC-8-200 MSA has an especially impressive level of capability, able to transit 200nm (370km) at 290kts (535 km/h), and then fly a low-level search track of about 1,000nm (1,851km) at 2,000ft (610m), making several target identifications, before returning to base with reserve fuel.

To allow better visual search by observers, DHC-8 MSAs are invariably fitted with domed observation blisters (favoured by PAL Aerospace) or enlarged conformal observation windows (used by Field). Field's conformal observation windows function as Type III emergency exits, and are optically flat, and do not distort the view for a camera. These are usually incorporated on an existing door or hatch, minimising structural modifications to the airframe.

In the maritime patrol role, there is frequently a requirement to drop items from the aircraft – including location- and smoke floats, oil sampling buoys and larger items such as inflatable life rafts. There may even be a requirement to paradrop personnel. If major modifications to the pressure cabin are to be avoided, this requires a door that can be opened in flight.

Field Aviation has a Federal Aviation Administration Supplemental Type Certificate (STC) for an air-operable rear door, which is incorporated on Japan and Swedish Coast Guard aircraft. The door (which is a modified version of the usual cargo door in the port rear fuselage) has airflow deflectors along the leading edge of the frame. Field insists that an air operable door gives a much better and more flexible solution than a drop hatch in the belly. There is

LEFT • *An airborne mission systems operator assigned to the 82nd Aerial Target Squadron, monitors a screen fed with the sea surveillance radar picture on an E-9A Widget. Either of the E-9As sweep the Gulf of Mexico, gather data, and send it to the range safety officer, allowing him or her to build the shoot pattern to safely test weapons during a Weapons System Evaluation Program.* US AIR FORCE/SENIOR AIRMAN DUSTIN MULLEN

BELOW •*ATK Integrated Systems of Fort Worth, Texas ordered the first and second of an eventual seven DHC-8-200 multi-role surveillance aircraft for the Air and Marine Office of the US Customs and Border Protection service. Aircraft N805MR is seen at the Fort Worth facility.* FIELD AVIATION

a clear limitation to the size of a hole that can reasonably be incorporated in the aircraft's underbelly, and the hatch occupies its own cabin space. An air operable door does not steal space from the cabin or cargo area, it provides an opening that is large enough (50 x 60in) for paratroopers and large size items.

Though a similar door is featured in artist's impressions of PAL's offering to the UAE Air Force, PAL has tended to emphasise the use of a drop hatch below the lower fuselage, and this has been used on aircraft used for the Netherlands Antilles contract.

Field Aviation designed and certified its own drop hatch for the Japan Coast Guard aircraft to meet a customer requirement for a hatch, in addition to an air operable door.

The key to any maritime surveillance aircraft lies in its mission systems and sensors, with an obvious requirement for sensors that can find and monitor objects of interest. Communication systems that allow the aircraft on patrol to co-ordinate its activities with other on-scene assets are also essential, to keep those on the ground fully informed and appraised, and to allow re-tasking of the aircraft in flight, if required. An advanced mission system is needed to integrate and fuse sensor information, and to allow a single operator to have a full picture and overview of the tactical situation. That operator needs a missionized crew-station, with controls and displays for communications

equipment and sensors.

The DHC-8 MSAs already in service use a range of sensors, including a 360° maritime surface search radar, and an infrared/electro-optical turret. Some aircraft also have side-looking airborne radar (SLAR).

Operators

The DHC-8 was first modified for the maritime patrol role in the mid-1990s when Field Aviation became involved in the Australian Customs Service Coastwatch programme. Field Aviation became an exclusive teaming partner with Surveillance Australia back in 1992 and developed the DHC-8 MPA with inputs from the customer in preparation for the Coastwatch tender – which was released in 1993. Surveillance Australia won the Australian Customs Service Coastwatch contract in the autumn of 1994. This resulted in three aircraft being ordered by Surveillance Australia, a subsidiary of National Air Support, which is itself part of Cobham Flight Operations & Services Australia. The aim of the programme was to provide airborne surveillance of the Australian Exclusive Economic Zone, searching for illegal fishing vessels, smugglers, and illegal immigrants and regular assistance in search and rescue operations.

The first three DHC-8 MPAs were delivered by Field from its Aviation Modification Centre at Toronto's Lester B. Pearson International Airport to Surveillance Australia in 1996, and the fleet was soon expanded to five DHC-8s

flying from three operational bases in Cairns, Darwin, and Broome.

In 2005, Surveillance Australia was awarded a further AUD $1bn Coastwatch contract to cover DHC-8 operations through to 2020. The fleet increased to ten aircraft, all equipped with new generation surveillance sensors, communications, and data management systems. Surveillance Australia was rebranded to Cobham Aviation Services Australia - Special Mission in 2009.

In November 2021 the Australian Department of Home Affairs approved a contract variation to extend the Surveillance Aircraft contract until December 31, 2027.

Eleven months later, Surveillance Australia was acquired by US defence contractor Leidos and is expected to be operated locally by Leidos Australia.

The Leidos Australia aircraft are equipped with Raytheon SeaVue surface search radars with additional inverse synthetic aperture radar, synthetic aperture radar and moving target indication capability. These are backed-up with advanced electro-optical sensors. The aircraft incorporate an Immarsat SATCOM system and a surveillance information management system, which integrates sensor data and provides real time communications to the Customs National Surveillance Centre in Canberra or to a mobile ground station.

Transport Canada operates three DHC-8 MSA aircraft fitted

RIGHT • *Operator stations fitted to a Swedish Coast Guard DHC-8-300.* FIELD AVIATION

with Swedish Space Corporation SLARs and mission management system, direction finding equipment, a Wescam MX-15 multi-spectral turret and conformal observation windows.

The three DHC-8 aircraft are used in support of the National Aerial Surveillance Programme to detect pollution from ships in waters under Canadian jurisdiction, especially in the busy commercial shipping lanes off Nova Scotia, Newfoundland, and Labrador. The aircraft now have the maritime surveillance system 6000, including SLAR, an ultraviolet infrared line scanner, an electro-optical infrared camera system, an automatic identification system for identifying shipping, a data link, and a geo-coded digital camera system comprising still and video cameras for documenting pollution incidents.

In 2000, Field Aviation responded to a request for information for a multi-

ABOVE • *Icelandic Coast Guard (Landhelgisaeslan) DHC-8-300 aircraft undertake maritime sovereignty patrol, environmental/pollution control, search and rescue, medevac, and transport duties.* FIELD AVIATION

LEFT • *In 2006, the Netherlands government signed a deal with Provincial Airlines of Canada, for the conversion of two DHC-8s for the maritime patrol role, for use by the Kustwacht voor de Nederlandse Antillen and Aruba.* PROVINCIAL AEROSPACE LIMITED

to convert the aircraft to MRSA configuration. ATK subsequently provided and installed its proprietary integrated intelligence, surveillance, and reconnaissance system, incorporating a Raytheon SeaVue surveillance radar, a Wescam MX-15 multi-spectral sensor and an integrated sensors and display system. These allow the CBP aircraft to detect activities of interest at substantial standoff range, and to transmit critical data and intelligence instantaneously to ground and airborne control centres. The aircraft's system also records the data and imagery, which can subsequently be used for intelligence, investigation, and prosecution.

Following Field Aviation's Australian and US Customs and Border Protection DHC-8 orders, the Kustbevakning (Swedish Coast Guard) ordered three new DHC-8-300 aircraft to replace its Casa 212s, signing a US $80m contract. The first of three aircraft was delivered to Field Aviation for modification on April 27, 2006, and was delivered to Skavsta Airport, south of Stockholm, on May 8, 2008.

The Swedish Coast Guard aircraft were fitted with an Elta maritime search radar, a Wescam MX-15 multi-spectral sensor, twin Swedish Space Corporation SLARs, and an infra-red/ultra-violet line scanner. This led to claims that the Kustbevakning aircraft had what was considered the most advanced maritime surveillance system available. The aircraft also featured Field Aviation's air operable door. The latter allows the aircraft to deploy location flares, oil sampling buoys and larger items such as inflatable life rafts, and pararescuemen when required.

The Japan Coast Guard selected the DHC-8-300 MSA in December 2006, with an initial requirement for three aircraft for maritime patrol and search and rescue duties within Japan's area of maritime responsibility. A first contract

was signed in January 2007, though subsequent orders for two and then three more aircraft in January 2008 and February 2009 brought the total to eight aircraft.

The aircraft were acquired from Bombardier Aerospace and modified by Field Aviation at its Toronto modification centre. They are equipped with a missionized interior, an air-operable rear cargo door and a fuselage drop hatch. The fuselage has a missionized, crew-station interior, and large, conformal observation windows.

Details of the mission system fitted to the Japanese aircraft are sketchy, though they are known to include a 360° surface search radar, a stabilised electro-optical turret, and a comprehensive suite of mission, navigation, and communications systems.

On May 7, 2007, Field Aviation signed a US $30m contract to supply the Landhelgisaeslan (Icelandic Coast Guard) with a new DHC-8-300 MSA. This was procured to replace the Icelandic Coast Guard's ageing Fokker F-27, and to fulfil what Georg Larusson, director general of the Icelandic Coast Guard, called "Growing airborne surveillance requirements to protect our fisheries interests and to fight environmental pollution."

The contract specified an aircraft similarly configured to the three DHC-8s delivered to the Swedish Coast Guard, lacking only the IR/UV scanner. The Icelandic MSA is a multi-mission aircraft, that undertakes maritime sovereignty patrol, environmental/pollution control, search and rescue, medevac, and transport duties.

The aircraft arrived at Field Aviation from Bombardier Aerospace on October 7, 2008, just as the last aircraft for Sweden was being prepared for its delivery flight.

Field Aviation's virtual monopoly of

role surveillance aircraft issued by the US Customs and Border Protection service. Field's response was based on the DHC-8-200 MPA as delivered to Surveillance Australia.

ATK Integrated Systems of Fort Worth, Texas ordered the first and second of an eventual seven DHC-8 multi-role surveillance aircraft, four DHC-8-200s and three DHC-8-300s. These aircraft were destined for the Air and Marine Office of the US Customs and Border Protection (an agency within the Department of Homeland Security) primarily to monitor drug trafficking and illegal immigration, and for search and rescue missions when required.

ATK Integrated Systems was the prime contractor, responsible for purchase of the aircraft, mission system integration and programme management. Field Aviation, ATK's primary subcontractor carried out the structural modifications and sensor integration required

RIGHT • *Nose-mounted searchlight installed on a DHC-8 belonging to the Kustwacht voor de Nederlandse Antillen and Aruba.* PROVINCIAL AEROSPACE LIMITED

maritime DHC-8 conversions came to an end in 2006, when the Netherlands government signed a deal with PAL Aerospace of Canada. The company converted two DHC-8s for the maritime patrol role, for use by the Kustwacht voor de Nederlandse Antilles & Aruba (KWNA&A, Coast Guard of the Netherlands Antilles and Aruba). Since the Netherlands Antilles (Curaçao, Bonaire, Sint Maarten, Sint Eustatius, and Saba) and Aruba lie close to the major drug trafficking routes from Colombia, the Kustwacht plays a vital role in counter-drugs operations, search and rescue and EEZ protection.

Until 2005, long-range maritime patrol on behalf of the KWNA&A was carried out by the Royal Netherlands Navy, which stationed two P-3C Orions at Hato Airport, Curacao. When the Netherlands government decided to sell its P-3C fleet, the UK stepped in to fill the breach, basing two RAF Nimrod MR2s in the region, before handing over to the Royal Netherlands Air Force, who deployed a pair of specially converted Fokker 60U aircraft.

KWNA&A used the Australian Coastwatch programme as a business model to contract Provincial Airlines to supply reconnaissance aircraft (which remained under the ownership of Provincial), crews, and services over a ten-year period. The two aircraft were modified with search radar, a nose-mounted searchlight, a FLIR turret, observation windows and an under-fuselage drop hatch, and were equipped with Provincial's airborne data acquisitions and management systems, a proprietary tactical management system. The aircraft entered service in the autumn of 2007.

Though the United Arab Emirates remains tight-lipped on details, the Emirates signed an AED 1.071bn contract with Provincial Aerospace to "supply modifications for two maritime patrol aircraft," in February 2009.

Provincial displayed a DHC-8-300 model in maritime configuration wearing UAE Air Force markings at the 2007 Dubai Air Show. The model was prominently placed in front of a poster advertising the Thales AMASCOS 300 airborne maritime situation control system – which had been a prominent feature of the CN235MPA configuration offered to the UAE.

The UAEAF DHC-8 MPAs are reportedly the most advanced versions in the world. Systems fitted are believed to include AMASCOS mission system, incorporating sensors and equipment from Thales (probably including Thales/ EADS Ocean Master 100 radar), surveillance equipment from Teledyne FLIR, electronic countermeasures equipment from Elettronica Spa, and secure telecommunications equipment from Rohde & Schwarz as well as unspecified items from Honeywell and from Saab Systems in South Africa (probably Saab Avitronics).

The DHC-8 model shown at the 2007 Dubai show featured the same nose mounted searchlight, under nose FLIR and belly mounted search radar and drop hatch as the aircraft modified by Provincial for the Netherlands Antilles and Aruba Coast Guard. The searchlight had been deleted from the models displayed at the International Defence Exhibition held in Abu Dhabi in March 2009, when the contract was announced covering two aircraft conversions. The aircraft were previously operated by Abu Dhabi Aviation as A6-ADF (msn 610) and A6-ADG (msn 624) and delivered to UAEAF as 1320 and 1321 in April 2012 and March 2012 respectively.

In addition to these maritime DHC-8s, there are other military, paramilitary and parapublic examples of the type. Some serve as transports and VIP transports, while others are used for flight checking and calibration.

BELOW • *The under-fuselage configuration of the E-9A aircraft which features a black radome and a white canoe, housing the antennas for the APS-143(V)1 Airborne Sea Surveillance Radar.* US AIR FORCE

ABOVE • *Transport Canada's DHC-8 C-GCFJ is one of two aircraft in operation, used for the National Aerial Surveillance Programme to detect pollution from ships in waters under Canadian jurisdiction.*
FIELD AVIATION

The Royal Canadian Air Force operates four aircraft used as navigation trainers (of six delivered) designated CT-142s, and the US Air Force uses a pair, designated as the E-9A Widget as range control platforms.

CT-142 Gonzo

Designed and produced in Canada, the CC-142 was a conversion of the DHC-8-100 twin turboprop regional airliner for military transport duties.

The DHC-8 designation covers a series of turboprop-powered regional airliners, originally introduced by de Havilland Canada (DHC) in 1984, and essentially derived from the DHC-7, albeit without the original aircraft's STOL capabilities.

DHC was later bought by Boeing in 1988, then by Bombardier in 1992, and finally by Longview Aviation Capital in 2019, who has revived the de Havilland Canada name and brand.

The first two CC-142 transports were delivered in March and May 1987, and, after company testing were used by a sub-unit of 412 Transport Squadron that was established at CFB Lahr in West Germany to support Canadian Forces in Europe. The two aircraft were used as utility transports and were painted in a two-tone green camouflage. Returning to Canada in 1993, the aircraft were assigned to 402 Squadron at CFB Winnipeg. By 1995, they had been painted in an overall grey finish.

The Winnipeg-based unit had replaced its DHC-3 Otters for nine Douglas CC-129 Dakotas in 1976, using them for light and VIP transport missions, search and rescue operations, and supporting the Canadian Forces SkyHawks Parachute Team. The squadron was the last unit in the Canadian Forces to fly the Dakota when the type was finally retired in 1988.

By then, a decision had been made that the next four DHC-8s would be delivered as navigation trainers, initially using the designation CC-142(N), and later CT-142, and affectionately nicknamed Gonzo because of its lengthened nose! Four aircraft were taken on strength between 1989 and 1991, modified by Bombardier for their new role.

The CT-142 Gonzo, features a suite of on board training computers, and a large nose mounted radar system with six consoles, allowing an instructor to student ratio of 2:4. The aircraft is augmented by a state-of-the-art ground based simulator, known as the tactical mission trainer, which is designed to give a seamless transition between ground based and airborne training.

Two CC-142 DHC-8 light transport aircraft were reported as being available for disposal in 1998 and were withdrawn and disposed of as part of wider force reductions. This left 402 Squadron just operating all four CT-142 Gonzo aircraft, in association with the Canadian Forces Air Navigation School (CFANS).

Named the 'City of Winnipeg' squadron, 402 Squadron, the squadron trains and qualifies Air Combat Systems Officers and Airborne Electronic Sensor Operators to support Royal Canadian Air Force (RCAF) requirements.

Originally delivered in an overall grey tactical paint scheme, the CT-142s subsequently received an overall blue colour scheme as per other aircraft within the NATO Flying Training Canada programme like the CT-155 Hawk and CT-156 Harvard II.

CFANS and 402 Squadron have continued Canada's long tradition of training Commonwealth aircrew, with students from the United Kingdom, Australia, and New Zealand training on the Gonzo, as well as allied aircrew from Germany and Norway. The client list also includes Singapore, the Republic of South Korea, and the United Arab Emirates.

In July 2019, PAL Aerospace was awarded a contract to provide heavy maintenance services for the Royal Canadian Air Force's CT-142 fleet. The contract covered an initial four-year period with potential for contract extensions that could increase the span of the agreement to seven years. PAL Aerospace performs the maintenance services required at its facilities in St John's, Newfoundland, and Winnipeg, Manitoba.

E-9A Widget

The 82nd Aerial Targets Squadron based at Tyndall Air Force Base, Florida operates two modified DHC-8s as range support aircraft under the designation E-9A. Known as Widgets, the E-9As were modified by Sierra Research and entered service in 1988. Equipped with an APS-143(V)1 Airborne Sea Surveillance Radar, the E-9s are used for surveillance and safety across the ranges located over the Gulf of Mexico. A large phased-array antenna enables the E-9A to simultaneously receive, record and downlink telemetry from aircraft, missiles, and other sources. The Widgets are also equipped with an over-the-horizon ultra-high frequency command, initiate and destruct relay system that permits the crew to destroy target drones and weapons should the need arise.

As fisheries and resource protection continue to increase in importance, and the need to counter piracy and illegal immigration gains an ever higher public prominence, prospects for further sales of DHC-8 MSAs seem bright, as an increasing number of countries seek cost effective solutions to their patrol and surveillance needs.

Polar Flyers

The British Antarctic Survey Air Unit plays a crucial role supporting research in Earth's last great wilderness. Mark Broadbent reports

Antarctica has been described as a place of superlatives. It is the highest, driest, coldest, and windiest continent on Earth. It has the harshest winter, with six months of darkness, and the planet's largest ice sheet that is three miles (4.8km) thick in places.

The continent has exerted a powerful hold on the imagination since its discovery in 1820. The quest to reach the South Pole, won in 1911 by the Norwegian explorer Roald Amundsen – who disappeared without trace in 1928 while piloting a rescue flight in the Arctic – was one of the greatest adventures of 20th century exploration.

Today, more than 60 years after the 1962 Antarctic Treaty laid out the conduct of the international presence and scientific research on the continent, the desire to understand Antarctica and its influence on our planet is undiminished. Its scale – it is roughly the size of the United States – and harsh climate means there are areas where nobody has ever visited, nor gone within 100 miles (160km) of.

Antarctica's forbidding terrain, brutal weather, and remoteness – it's more than 1,100 miles (1,770km) away from the nearest population centre – means air support is critical in providing the supply and logistics lifelines to the frozen continent.

Antarctic Air Unit

The British Antarctic Survey (BAS) is an environmental research centre headquartered in Cambridge that's responsible for the UK's national scientific activities on the continent. The BAS established an Air Unit in the 1960s to provide dedicated support for its operations. It was initially staffed by Royal Air Force pilots before civilian aviators gradually took over from the early 1970s. It currently flies four de Havilland Canada DHC-6 Twin Otters and a single DHC Dash 7, all resplendent in a distinctive black and red livery.

The Twin Otters currently in service were all purchased directly from the manufacturer during the 1980s and the Dash has been used since 1994. All five are registered in the Falkland Islands, a British Overseas Territory, with regulatory oversight provided

BELOW • *The BAS Dash 7 provides the intercontinental link to Rothera from South America.* GRAEME NOTT VIA BRITISH ANTARCTIC SURVEY

by Air Safety Support International, a wholly owned subsidiary of the UK Civil Aviation Authority.

The Twin Otters are currently maintained by Rocky Mountain Aircraft in Calgary and the Dash 7 by Voyageur Airways at North Bay near Toronto, Ontario. The aircraft are ferried from Canada to Antarctica by the Air Unit's eight pilots in time for the start of the polar summer in October. The aircraft operate there until the end of the season in March before returning to Canada. Darkness and severe cold prevent flying at all other times of the year.

Intercontinental Dash
The centre of the BAS Air Unit's operations is the Rothera Research Station on the Antarctic Peninsula. Rothera has a 2,952ft (900m) gravel runway, hangars, maintenance facilities and an operations tower, which provides a 360° view to help ensure the safe passage of flights in and out of the airfield.

The Dash 7 transports passengers, food, spare parts and some scientific equipment to Rothera from Mount Pleasant Airfield in the Falklands and Punta Arenas in southern Chile, which are respectively 1,000nm (1,860km) and 880nm (1,630km) away. The flights are dependent on the weather and are only permitted when there are good conditions at a diversion airport on the Antarctic Peninsula.

The Dash is important to the BAS because it flies people and supplies from South America to Rothera in around five-and-a-half hours instead of the four days to two weeks it can take to get there by ship. Poor weather and sea ice means ships don't get into Rothera until mid-December, the middle of the Antarctic summer. The rapid and frequent link provided by these flights

(which take place every two weeks on average), "attracts high-profile scientists to BAS", said Rod Arnold, head of the Air Unit, in an interview with the author.

The Dash has several modifications from the type's standard configuration to enable it to conduct this intercontinental air-bridge role, including long-range fuel tanks with a jettison system, a large cargo door and a strengthened cargo floor. The aircraft seats up to 16 passengers and can carry up to 4,409lb (2,000kg) of cargo on these flights.

Into the Continent
From Rothera, personnel and equipment are taken deeper into Antarctica, to the Halley Research Station, 900nm (1,666km) away to the northeast across the Weddell Sea, or to the Sky-Blu Logistics Facility, which is 400nm (814km) to the southeast. Sky-Blu has a 3,937ft (1,200m) groomed blue ice runway, permanently marked by flags, that's suitable for wheeled aircraft.

The Twin Otters are equipped with both wheels and skis which enable operations from Rothera's gravel strip, the blue ice at Sky-Blu and

LEFT • ADAM BRADLEY/
BRITISH ANTARCTIC SURVEY

snow. The Dash only operates between Rothera and Sky-Blu. Being able to fly the Dash there provides major operational benefits. "You can fly direct from Rothera with a payload of 8,500lb [3,855kg], drop it off and return having used no fuel in the field, and you've done that in something like five-and-a-half hours," Arnold explained.

In comparison, it takes the Twin Otters a full day to do the same journey (with a fuel stop at the Fossil Bluff Logistics Facility on George VI Sound), carrying 1,800lb (816kg).

Field Research
Once at Halley or Sky-Blu, the research parties and everything they'll need to survive and work – the specially-designed pyramid tents able to withstand ferocious winds and wind-driven ice particles, as well as food, fuel, skidoos, sledges, and scientific equipment – are flown to remote field research camps by the Twin Otters. Typically, two or three of these aircraft are forward-deployed from Rothera to Halley and Sky-Blu for these tasks.

These aircraft are also used to re-supply the field camps, return scientists once they've completed their research, maintain equipment at remote unmanned sensing stations and lay depots and fuel stockpiles for future field parties.

The Twin Otter's rugged construction, renowned short take-off, and landing (STOL) performance in remote environments is ideal for this type of flying. The skis take away some of the

aircraft payload as they weigh close to 800lb (363kg), so the BAS' Twin Otters have an increased gross weight of 14,000lb (6,350kg) compared to the type's standard 12,500lb (5,670kg). That gives the aircraft a useful cargo and fuel payload without compromising range.

Airborne Science
The Air Unit's aircraft are more than just transport workhorses. Two of the Twin Otters (VP-FAZ and VP-FBL) are instrumented with airborne surveying and remote sensing equipment to help scientists investigate Antarctica's ice and geology.

VP-FAZ is a Meteorological Airborne Science Instrumentation (MASIN) aircraft used to study boundary layers and cloud. It is fitted with temperature and water vapour sensors and a turbulence probe (which take detailed measurements of temperature, dew point and winds), radiation instruments and a downwards-looking infrared thermometer. The wing pylons carry a cloud and aerosol spectrometer, water vapour and carbon dioxide sensors, an optical particle counter and a cloud condensation nuclei counter.

Remote Sensing
Twin Otter VP-FBL is instrumented for airborne geophysics, which involves remotely sensing the ice and the rocks deep below. Ice-penetrating radar pulses radio waves that bounce back from the rock below the ice sheet, helping build a picture of both the ice and the nature of the rocks beneath it.

This aircraft has wingtip-mounted magnetometers (to measure the strength and direction of magnetic fields) and a gravity system, which assesses the minute differences in the Earth's gravitational field caused by the varying density of the rocks. The Dash can also carry wingtip magnetometers and the gravity system for aerial surveys.

Missions are flown along a grid pattern to systematically cover a pre-planned survey area. Dr Tom Jordan, an aero geophysicist, explained to the author: "If you've got a rock under the ice that's

BELOW • PETE
BUCKTROUT/BRITISH
ANTARCTIC SURVEY

RIGHT • *The Rothera hangar is the BAS Air Unit's base in Antarctica.*
PETE BUCKTROUT/BRITISH ANTARCTIC SURVEY

BELOW RIGHT • PETE BUCKTROUT/BRITISH ANTARCTIC SURVEY

full of lots of magnetic minerals, it will act as an amplifier, making the earth's magnetic field stronger as you fly over that particular point.

"If you fly over a rock type that's got no magnetic minerals in it the magnetic field will be lower. By flying the grid pattern, we can join together all our measurements to build up a map of how strong the magnetic field is and what that tells us about the geology under the ice."

Other systems can be mounted in the Twin Otters' floor hatch openings as research needs dictate. These include a laser range finder to measure ice floe topography, video and digital SLR cameras to provide visual references for the data sets or count birds, penguins and seals, and a hyperspectral suite of imaging equipment for geology or vegetation studies. Airborne sensors can also be dropped through the hatches or towed behind the aircraft.

Normally research flights are flown by a single pilot and one operator. The latter sits in the back controlling the sensors and viewing the read-outs they provide using a control console or tablet computer. The BAS survey network lets multiple operators view and use the equipment installed on the aircraft.

Discoveries

VP-FBL has helped with significant discoveries in Antarctica. In January 2014, British scientists announced they'd found a trough deeper than the Grand Canyon in the Ellsworth Subglacial Highlands, an ancient mountain range in West Antarctica under several miles of ice. The readings from the aircraft's radar gathered during survey flights, alongside satellite data, determined the Ellsworth Trough, as the feature was named, is 1.8 miles (3km) deep, more than 186 miles (300km) long and up to 15 miles (25km) wide in places.

In the 2008 and 2009 summer seasons, VP-FBL was used as part of a multinational research programme to map the Gamburtsev Subglacial Mountains, a range in Eastern Antarctica hidden under 2.4 miles (4km) of ice. The Gamburtsevs were discovered by Soviet scientists in 1958 but the Twin Otter's remote-sensing technology helped to reveal, for the first time, the detail of a jagged landscape with sharp peaks as high as 9,186ft (2,800m) and valleys as deep as 2,624ft (800m).

Dr Jordan described the experience of flying over the ice during these flights: "The pilot can look out of the aircraft and see flat white as far as the eye can see. By looking at my screen inside [which provides read-outs from the radar], I can tell him that he's flying over a mountain range the size of the Alps that's completely covered by ice."

Dash Upgrade

Antarctica has unique operational challenges (see the Antarctic Flying panel) and, to ensure it remains fit for its role, in 2010 the Dash's cockpit was upgraded in Canada by Voyageur

LEFT • *A glaciologist uses ground-based GPS and the Twin Otter to survey the flow of the ice sheet*
DAVID VAUGHAN/ BRITISH ANTARCTIC SURVEY

Antarctic Flying

Antarctica is one of the most demanding places to fly on Earth. The weather, terrain, operating in the field with no support and flying into areas that have never been landed on before, poses a unique operational challenge. "There are some areas where you can fly for five hours and see nothing but white, which has a certain beauty on its own, but also there are some spectacular mountain regions," said Alan Meredith, the BAS Air Unit's then chief pilot. "Each has its challenges. There's the issue of whiteout in the flat white nothingness and the challenges of mountain flying. It's a spectacular place to fly and the photographs you see don't do it justice."

BAS Air Unit operations are supported by a weather forecaster at Rothera, seconded from the UK Met Office, who uses real-time weather data generated by a satellite ground station. "We use the technology to plan ahead," said Rod Arnold, head of the Air Unit. "It enables us to not leave our aircraft out exposed to big storms. We can move our aircraft to miss out on the worst of

the conditions and make the best use of weather windows."

Meredith said pilots flying in the Antarctic require certain qualities: "You need to be self-reliant, have a huge amount of common sense and know when to stop. You've got to be level-headed and think ahead. You must be able to imagine what could go wrong and put things in place to ensure it doesn't.

As with all BAS staff heading to Antarctica, the pilots complete first aid and field training courses in the UK before they go. Once they arrive, the pilots undergo an extensive training programme to learn about flying in the environment. With BAS Twin Otter operations being single-pilot there's a building-block approach to steadily increase expertise.

"First we teach them to fly on skis, then we send them out on training sectors with another pilot then give them runs delivering fuel," Meredith explained. "After that we send them out as a single pilot but with another aircraft so they're not on their own. They gradually build up to being fully qualified in mountain flying. It takes two years to get them to where they can

walk into a briefing in the morning, and they'll be able to do 95% of tasks on the tasking board."

The Air Unit currently has eight pilots. They have a variety of backgrounds including bush flying, airlines, survey work, instructing and operating fast jet and transport aircraft in the military. This wide spectrum of experience provides strengths in different areas, enabling the Air Unit to conduct a variety of assignments ranging from intercontinental flying with the Dash 7 to operating from unprepared landing strips at field camps with the Twin Otters.

The broad experience base also helps maximise safety. "People are willing to share both good and bad experiences," Meredith explained. "They're more likely to ask for help if they need it and listen to people around them."

"In Antarctica," he added, "it's important that people aren't scared of asking if they're unsure, reporting when it goes wrong and happy discussing among their peers. Building a safe environment is key because everything you do in Antarctica carries a greater risk than equivalent activities elsewhere."

LEFT • *A BAS Twin Otter undergoing refuelling at the Sky-Blu ice runway under the midnight sun.*
JOHN DUDENEY VIA BRITISH ANTARCTIC SURVEY

RIGHT • *A BAS Twin Otter flying low over a striking crevasse field.*
PETER CONVEY/BRITISH ANTARCTIC SURVEY

Airways, an operator and maintenance organisation, to enhance crews' situational awareness.

The updated cockpit features four large-format Universal Avionics EFI-890R flat panel displays and specialised flight management systems. The latter includes multi-mission management software, terrain awareness and warning and synthetic vision systems, radio control units, application server units for charts and checklists, and an electronic document display.

Alan Meredith, BAS' then chief pilot, said at the time that the upgrade, "future proofed this airframe for which there is no obvious alternative that meets the BAS' operating criteria". The lack of another type which, like the Dash, can fly intercontinental services but still has STOL capabilities, means there's a question mark over how the Air Unit will maintain the vital air-bridge to Antarctica in the future.

The Dash 7 has been out of production since 1988 and the worldwide fleet has now reduced to 32 aircraft out of the 115 built. The declining user base and a shrinking spares pool will mean the aircraft will become less cost-effective to operate in the long term, Arnold said.

The Twin Otters are slightly different. "We're nowhere near the life of the fuselages, we only use around 600

flying hours per year, and you can re-life [parts], so they're good for the foreseeable future," Arnold said. He added that the wings of the highest flight hour aircraft are scheduled for replacement in around two years' time.

This will be the first structural modification on the Twin Otter fleet in 32 years of operations, a testament to the type's durability. With over 600 Twin Otters in use and the type still being built (in Series 400 guise, by Viking Air),

spares stocks are plentiful, and support is comprehensive. Operating the Twin Otter will continue to be cost-effective for many more years of operations in Antarctica.

Involvement of these aircraft in mapping the Gamburtsevs and finding the Ellsworth Trough highlight the BAS Air Unit's importance in helping scientists understand Antarctica and making possible exploration of the desolate, beautiful ice continent.

Canada's Firefighter

Viking Aircraft is enhancing the CL-415 and development of its aerial firefighter might not stop there. Mark Broadbent reports

ABOVE • VIKING AIR LTD

In June 2016, Viking Aircraft of British Colombia announced a major development - the acquisition of the type certificates and manufacturing rights for all variants of Bombardier's amphibious aircraft.

The acquisition, following Bombardier's strategic decision to focus on airliners and business jets, meant Viking assumed responsibility for all product support, parts and maintenance activities on the worldwide fleet of Bombardier aerial firefighters – the CL-415 and variants and its CL-215 piston-engine and CL-215T turboprop predecessors – from a newly acquired, specially repurposed 50,000ft2 (4,645m2) facility in Calgary, Alberta.

The deal further strengthened the Canadian company's specialism of providing product support for legacy de Havilland Canada/Canadair commercial piston and turboprop aircraft, after earlier acquiring the Beaver, Otter, Twin Otter, Buffalo, and DHC-7 type certificates from Bombardier.

Nearly two years later, in May 2018, Viking announced the next step in its management of the amphibious aircraft range: the launch of the CL-415 Enhanced Aerial Firefighter (CL-415EAF) conversion programme to upgrade legacy CL-215 and C-215T aerial firefighters.

The CL-415EAF is significant not just because it introduces new features to a legacy product, but also because it is

a bridge to a potential new-production aerial firefighter.

Amphibian Ancestry

There is a long history of producing specialist amphibious aerial firefighting aircraft in Canada. The original CL-215 powered by two Pratt & Whitney Twin Wasp R-2800 radial engines flew in 1967 and entered service with the Sécurité Civile (French Civil Protection Agency) two years later. Production ended in 1990.

The CL-215T, a turbine retrofit introducing Pratt & Whitney Canada PW123AF turboprops to replace the Wasps was launched in 1987 (first flight 1989, initial delivery 1991), with two CL-215s converted to function as

development and demonstrator aircraft. However, a decision was made not to continue with retrofit kits for this aircraft as the market was favouring new-builds. The new CL-415 was launched in 1991, with the aircraft flying in December 1993 and first delivery in November 1994.

According to Viking Aircraft, at the time of launching the new CL-415 there were 170 CL-215/CL-215T/CL-415-family aerial firefighters in service worldwide. They are operational in Canada, Croatia, France, Greece, Italy, Malaysia, Morocco, Portugal, Spain, Thailand, Turkey, and the United States, with both air forces and para-public organisations operating the aircraft.

A Viking spokesperson told the author: "The CL family of aircraft is very robust. It's able to go into a high sea state and is built for severe operating environments. Unlike a lot of aircraft, the CL family do not have life limits on the airframe. They are the only aerial firefighters in the world with full OEM [original equipment manufacturer] support, designed specifically for aerial firefighting and working that amphibious saltwater environment."

Enhanced Aerial Firefighter

The CL-415EAF is the next evolution of Canada's aerial firefighter. The programme is a collaboration between Viking and its sister company Longview Aviation Asset Management (LAAM), a Calgary-based organisation established in 2016 to provide financing, lease

options and trade-in capabilities for aircraft supported and manufactured by Viking.

The CL-415EAF introduced several airframe and systems improvements. Electrical, fuel, hydraulic and flight control systems are upgraded, and customers can choose from options that include an external engine wash system, an enlarged cargo door and a ground auxiliary power unit to run the aircraft's electrical systems and charge the batteries for engine starting.

The upgrade confronts issues caused by ageing parts in older airframes and improves maintainability. A Viking spokesperson told the author: "With all the worldwide obsolescence we're seeing today, we make sure the

CL-415 Enhanced Aerial Firefighter Characteristics

Wingspan	28.6m (93ft 8in)
Height	8.92m (29ft 2in)
Length	19.82m (65ft)
Max take-off weight	19,731kg (43,499lb) disposable load
Water tank capacity	5,450lit (1,439 US gal)
Cabin volume	35.5m^3 (1,253ft^3)
Take-off distance (land)	Not available
Take-off distance (water)	Not available
Landing distance (land)	Not available
Landing distance (water)	Not available
Minimum water depth	Not available
Ferry range	1,310nm
Powerplant	Two Pratt & Whitney Canada PW123AF turboprops, generating 2,380shp (1,775kW) each
Crew	2

in-service operators are not worried about operational deficiencies."

This approach is in line with Viking's primary activity of providing product support for the legacy de Havilland Canada/Canadair commercial aircraft. A Viking spokesperson explained: "We do all the modifications relevant to the aircraft in airworthiness, engineering support, field services reps, spares, customisations, repair; everything you think of as a normal OEM like Airbus, Boeing, Bombardier, the same [goes] for Viking."

Another key part of tackling obsolescence is to ensure that avionics are modernised to improve functionality and comply with existing and upcoming regulatory requirements. On the CL-415EAF there will be several new standard flight deck features: GPS, a traffic collision and avoidance system, a terrain awareness warning system, automatic dependent surveillance-broadcast out, a flight management

system (FMS) and flight director. Final supplier selection to provide the avionics is currently underway.

Customers can choose from optional extras, including synthetic vision, a flight data recorder, a dual radio altimeter, a VHF radio/data link, a Link 2000+ controller-pilot data link, aircraft communications addressing and reporting system, a dual FMS/GPS, a satcom automated flight information reporting system and weather radar. Further avionics options include an enhanced autopilot, a head-up display, and a night-vision imaging system.

The Viking spokesperson said: "We'll also be enhancing water-carrying and dropping capabilities." The CL-415EAF will have a 5,450lit (1,439 US gal) tank, the capability to drop foam-injected water retardant and the ability to scoop a complete tank-load from any suitable water source in just 12 seconds. Viking says the aircraft can drop up to 125,000lit (33,021 US gal) per hour.

Like the CL-215 and CL-415, the CL-415EAF features winglets and finlets, has a higher maximum take-off weight, component improvements and corrosion protection enhancements and a flight deck air conditioning system.

Producing the Aircraft

Eleven CL-215s owned by LAAM have been earmarked to enter the CL-415EAF conversion programme. The first converted aircraft was completed in 2020. A Viking spokesperson said: "LAAM will be doing the physical conversions of the aircraft, Viking will be supplying the kits and the parts and maintaining all the support required for airworthiness – product support [and] technical support in the field."

To initiate the programme, LAAM hired technical and support staff members for its Calgary facilities and Viking recruited other staff for its Victoria facilities to support development of the conversion kits. Viking also reinstated its Viking Academy programme to provide the specialist technical training required for these positions.

Both LAAM and Viking are also working with local institutions, including the Southern Alberta Institute of Technology, to develop innovative technologies and provide training assistance to support the programme, and Viking has partnerships with

companies participating in the British Columbia Technology Super Cluster initiative.

New Opportunities

During its time managing the CL-415 programme, Bombardier developed a maritime patrol version of the aircraft, the CL-415MP. Two examples of this variant serve with the Malaysian Maritime Enforcement Agency undertaking surveillance and SAR missions, with the aircraft equipped with a side-looking airborne radar, radio direction finder, an electro-optical/infrared sensor, an automatic identification system, digital data and video recording and a high-speed satellite data link.

A Viking spokesperson said: "We're finding operators don't just want to use an asset for firefighting, but for other jobs during the year or during the [fire] season when they're not required. That's where the avionics suite becomes important; those things change the dynamic of the aircraft."

To this end, the CL-415EAF is pitched as an aircraft that can not only operate as a firefighter but can also carry specialist role equipment and therefore be re-tasked for other missions. For example, the aircraft has a large cargo door for transport missions and a stretcher rack for emergency medical services, and the ability to carry a spray boom system for pollution control work.

The Viking spokesperson said: "The intention is to open the CL-415EAF to new markets. Using new components to reduce maintenance and training costs is important in this regard, as adding improvements to an established platform is meant to appeal to operators in secondary markets that can't afford an all-new next-generation aircraft and the costs associated with it."

Like Viking's other amphibious aircraft, the CL-415EAF is supported by the company's Maintenance Plus programme, which supplies operators with components at a fixed yearly fee plus a fixed rate per flight hour. The objectives are to provide customers with a good availability rate from the very start of operations, guarantee spares availability, provide better maintenance planning and predictable spares costs, and eliminate yearly maintenance expenditure fluctuations.

Viking says Maintenance Plus provides reduced aircraft operating costs, assurances for operators over the cost of parts consumption,

ABOVE • *On November 1, 2022, President Macron of France announced that by the end of his term in 2027 the country will have replaced its 12 Canadair CL-215 scooping air tankers and increased the number to 16. The DHC-515 is a leading contender.* VIKING AIR LTD

advance awareness of parts maintenance, increased buying power by consolidating operators' parts forecasts to obtain the best possible prices, and a unique maintenance plan compiled from the collective knowledge of all customers.

On March 11, 2020, the first CL-415EAF C-GFBN (msn 1081) had made its inaugural flight at Abbotsford, British Colombia following modification by Cascade Aerospace using a conversion kit and manufacturing support from Viking Air Ltd. A CL-415EAF is a selected CL-215 airframe converted to turbine configuration using Viking-supplied conversion kits. Bridger Aerospace based at Bozeman, Montana was the CL-415EAF's launch customer with a 2018 order and options for up to six aircraft which were all exercised. The first aircraft was delivered in April 2020.

DHC-515

Conversion of CL-215 aircraft into CL-415EAFs established a new production standard and reactivated the supply chain, which in turn established a footing for Viking to produce a new-generation

amphibious aerial firefighter called the CL-515.

Following an extensive business and technical review on March 31, 2022, De Havilland Aircraft of Canada Ltd launched the DHC-515 Firefighter, formerly known as the CL-515.

At the time, European customers had signed letters of intent to purchase the first 22 DHC-515 aircraft pending government-to-government negotiations through the Government of Canada's contracting agency, the Canadian Commercial Corporation (CCC).

De Havilland Canada expects to deliver the first DHC-515 aircraft by the middle of the decade. Final assembly takes place in Calgary, Alberta where work on the CL-215 and CL- 415 aircraft currently takes place.

A Viking spokesperson said the CL-415EAF and the CL-515 fill a niche: "Every other aerial firefighter is a modification through supplemental type certificates. This is the only aircraft designed to do that job. It's robust, it's very efficient, it's a workhorse."

On November 1, 2022, President Macron announced that by the end of his term in 2027 France will have replaced its 12 Canadair CL-215

scooping air tankers and increased the number to 16 with an investment of €250m. The DHC-515 is a leading contender.

DHC-515 Firefighter Facts

- Can deliver multiple drops, in rapid succession, meaning faster fire suppression.
- Can deliver 700,000lit of water into the fire-zone per day.
- Refills its tanks in 12 seconds, from nearby fresh or saltwater sources including rivers, small lakes, and oceans.
- Equipped with a high-lift wing and turboprop engines that provided instant thrust, allow for safer operation in mountainous terrain and the ability to drop close to fire with superior precision.
- Performs in high winds typical with megafires, capable of refilling in rough waters with waves up to two metres caused by the high winds.
- Turboprop engines produce up to 50% lower CO_2 emissions and burn 25% to 40% less fuel than jet engines.
- The DHC-515 is the only aerial firefighter aircraft fully supported by the Original Equipment Manufacturer and comes with complementary full life-cycle support services.

The Super Tucano

David Willis details the development and operators of the EMB-314 Super Tucano, the most successful turboprop light attack aircraft in production today

The Super Tucano was developed from the EMB-312 Tucano, with greater emphasis on air-to-ground and anti-helicopter roles, as well as the interception of slow, fixed-wing aircraft, than the earlier design. It also built on experience gained from the Short Tucano programme for the Royal Air Force (RAF), whose aircraft were powered by a more powerful engine than the Pratt & Whitney Canada PT6A-25C used by the original Tucano. Although designed as a basic trainer, the Tucano earned an enviable reputation in combat operations, with for example, Colombia operating the aircraft against guerrillas operating in the country and intercepting drug-smuggling aircraft in its airspace. This alerted Embraer to a new potential market for a refined version of the Tucano with greater power, more armament options and better equipment for combat missions.

From the late 1980s, Embraer began to study a Super Tucano as the EMB-312F, with F standing for future. It incorporated some features of the Short-built aircraft, including the airbrake, while more powerful versions of the PT6A and the Garrett TPE331 engines were considered. Following the sale of Tucanos to the French Air Force as the EMB-312F (F for France), the project was retitled the EMB-312H Super Tucano.

A production Tucano airframe was modified with a 1.31m (4ft 31/2in) extension to the rear fuselage and an airbrake, while a 1,250shp (930kW) PT6A-67 engine was installed. The modified aircraft completed its first flight in the new configuration on September 9, 1991. A further pair of prototypes was built two years later, incorporating a new cockpit layout with a revised canopy and a 1,300shp (956kW) PT6A-68A turboprop.

Launch Customer

Interest in the project was soon expressed by the Força Aérea Brasileira (FAB, Brazilian Air Force), which was seeking an aircraft to intercept illegal flights and for the light attack role in the Amazon under the proposed Sistema de Vigilância da Amazônia (SIVAM, Amazon Surveillance System) programme. The EMB-312H was also considered as a

BELOW • *Embraer's corporate colours for the A-29 Super Tucano.* EMBRAER

replacement for the EMB-326 Xavante trainers flown by Esquadrão 'Joker', the 2°/5° Grupo de Aviação (GAv), based at Natal Air Base.

A contract was signed on August 18, 1995, for 100 EMB-312Hs for the FAB, comprising 50 single-seat A-29As (with a fuel tank in the rear cockpit) and 50 two-seat A-29Bs. Several changes to the design were requested by the FAB, which were incorporated into the prototypes. They included adding an additional pair of underwing pylons (for a total of five), and the ability to use smart weapons and two Mectron MAA-1 Piranha air-to-air missiles. The cockpit was revised, with Martin-Baker Mk10LCX ejection seats; new avionics with dual liquid-crystal displays and a head-up display, all compatible with night-vision goggles, plus a helmet-mounted display; ultra- and very high frequency tactical radios; a hands-on-throttle-and-stick (HOTAS) flight control system; a GPS inertial navigation system, and dual-axis autopilot. The aircraft would also be able to carry a forward-looking infrared sensor and be protected by radar and missile warning systems.

Flight testing resulted in a further series of alterations during 1998. They included a redesigned wing, a reinforced landing gear, further changes to the canopy, a greater weapons capacity and installation of a pair of 12.7mm (0.5in) machine guns, each with 200 rounds.

More power was also required, leading to the installation of the PT6A-68/3 rated at 1,600shp (1,193kW), while the intake was redesigned to

protect the engine from debris while operating from unprepared airstrips. The resulting aircraft was designated the EMB-314 Super Tucano (YA-29 by FAB), making its first flight on June 2, 1999.

An order for 76 aircraft, plus 23 more initially as options (later firmed up), was placed by the FAB on August 8, 2001. The 99 aircraft were delivered as 33 A-29As and 66 A-29Bs. The first was handed over on December 18, 2003, and all 99 were with the FAB by June 2012.

As of February 2023, Brazil's Super Tucano are assigned to four operational squadrons (which use a mix of A-29As and Bs); 1°/3° GAv 'Escorpião' of Ala (Wing) 7 at Boa Vista; 2°/3° GAv 'Grifo' of Ala 6 at Porto Velho; and 3°/3° GAv 'Flecha' of Ala 5 at Campo Grande.

They undertake light attack operations and intercept aircraft operating illegally in, or entering, Brazilian airspace, as well as surveillance missions. Two-seat A-29Bs are also used as trainers by 2°/5° GAv 'Joker' of Ala 10 at Natal.

The last – and most famous – Brazilian operator is the Esquãdrao de Demonstração Aérea (EDA, Air Demonstration Squadron, also known as Esquadrilha da Fumaça or 'Smoke Squadron'), the FAB's display team. It received the first of eight Super Tucanos from October 1, 2012, to replace its T-27 Tucanos.

Brazilian Super Tucanos have been used on operations against illegal runways, destroying them with bombs, and to intercept unidentified aircraft crossing the country's borders, most of which are involved in the narcotics trade. In some cases, the A-29s have shot down the intruders, while in other

engagements the intruders were forced to land. The A-29s operate alongside Embraer R-99A airborne early warning aircraft in conjunction with ground-based radar stations, which are used to control operations over the Amazon. They are responsible for guiding the Super Tucanos towards any suspicious aircraft.

The main weapon used by Brazilian Super Tucanos during such interception operations are their internal guns.

For air-to-ground missions the A-29 can employ M117, Mk81, Mk82 and Mk83 bombs, or pods for seven 70mm (2.7in) rockets, while for training sorties the SUU-20 with four 70mm rockets and six BDU-33 practice bombs can be carried. The FAB tested a GPS guidance kit developed by Britanite for the Mk81, Mk82 and Mk83 bombs, as well as the Israeli Lizard laser-guided bomb, but neither were adopted for operational use by the air force. In 2013, Embraer submitted a proposal to integrate a P-Band (synthetic aperture radar) reconnaissance pod developed by Orbisat.

The Super Tucano can carry a wide variety of external stores; by mid-2011 a total of 133 different external stores configurations had been qualified, with many more since. Some of the many other weapons that can be carried by the Super Tucano include the AIM-9 Sidewinder and Rafael Python 3/4 air-to-air missiles; AGM-65 Maverick air-to-surface missile; Israel Military Industries Delilah loitering munition; Paveway laser-guided bombs; GBU-38 and GBU-54 Joint Direct Attack Munitions; and the GBU-39 Small Diameter Bombs.

LEFT • *An artist's rendering of an A-29B Super Tucano loaded with a 70mm rocket pod and a single Joint Direct Attack Munition on the under-wing pylons.* EMBRAER

Export Success

The Super Tucano has achieved considerable success in the export market, appealing to nations that do not need, or cannot afford, sophisticated jet combat aircraft. It has entered service with air forces in Latin America, Africa, and Asia, as well as being selected for licence assembly in the United States by the Sierra Nevada Corporation (SNC) for the US Air Force and partner nations.

Initial interest came from nations in Latin America, with Colombia becoming the first overseas air force to receive Super Tucanos. An order for 25 was announced in December 2005, with the first five delivered one year later and the last entering service in August 2008. In service, the aircraft (serial numbers FAC 3101 to FAC 3125) were assigned to the Escuadrón de Combates (Combat Squadrons) 211, 312 and 611, although 211's aircraft were reassigned to the Grupo Aéreo de Casanare (Casanare Air Group) in October 2017. Colombia's Super Tucanos have seen extensive combat, fighting the Fuerzas Armadas Revolucionarias de Colombia (FARC, Revolutionary Armed Forces of Colombia) and other groups, as detailed below.

Although it was the second overseas customer to receive Super Tucanos, the Dominican Republic was the first to place an order for the aircraft, announcing a deal for 10 on August 20, 2001. The order was later abandoned, but the Super Tucano was again selected by Dominica in late 2008 and the first of eight was delivered on December 18, 2009. The last was handed over in October 2010. The

aircraft (serial numbers FAD 2900 to 2907) entered service with Escuadrón de Combate 'Dragones' (Combat Squadron 'Dragons') at San Isidro Air Base.

Chile received the first of 12 Super Tucanos in December 2009, having selected the type for the light attack and training roles to replace Cessna A-37B Dragonflies and some of its ENAER/CASA 101 fleet. The aircraft were the initial Super Tucanos with a full glass cockpit, featuring an additional screen over the two previously standard. Its aircraft were assigned to Grupo de Aviacion N°1 (1st Aviation Group) at Base Aérea 'Los Cóndores' in Iquique. Chile ordered a second batch of six in October 2017, which were delivered from March 2018, while a further four were delivered in late 2020 for a total of 22.

Ecuador signed for 24 Super Tucanos in 2008, although the commitment was later reduced by six. The initial

pair arrived in the country on January 24, 2010, replacing A-37Bs of Ala de Combate 23 (Combat Air Wing 23) at Manta Air Base in the second quarter of 2011. The wing has two flying units, Escuadrón de Combates (Combat Squadrons) 2311 'Dragones' and 2313 'Halcones'. The aircraft (serial numbers FAE 1010 to 1027) are equipped with a forward-looking infrared sensor, while they are armed with Lizard laser-guided bombs, 70mm rockets and free-fall weapons. Ecuador lost a Super Tucano (FAE 1016) on March 19, 2012, following engine failure during take-off.

Several other Latin America nations expressed interest in the Super Tucano but did not take delivery. El Salvador wanted up to 10 in late 2010, but no order was announced. From early 2011 Peru investigated acquiring 12 Super Tucanos but selected the Korea Aerospace Industries KT-1 instead the following year. In the second half of 2011 Guatemala sought finance for

LEFT • *An A-29A in the colour scheme used by the Força Aérea Brasileira* EMBRAER

RIGHT • *Two A-29Bs each loaded with external fuel tanks both painted in Embraer corporate colours* EMBRAER

BELOW RIGHT • *Air-to-air missiles have been cleared for use from the Super Tucano, although they are rarely carried in service. This aircraft is one of the two prototypes produced by Embraer* EMBRAER

six aircraft, resulting in a deal being finalised in April 2013. Although the order was cancelled in November 2013, a requirement for two aircraft was revealed in early 2015, but again not fulfilled. The Super Tucano was selected by Paraguay in May 2012, but no order materialised. Honduras sought to acquire between eight and 12 in early 2012, reduced to five in mid-2014, with an order for two announced in October 2014. Bolivia also expressed an interest in the Super Tucano during November 2017.

Four countries in Africa have acquired Super Tucanos from Embraer. Burkina Faso was the seventh nation to purchase the aircraft, receiving three (registrations XT-MEA to XT-MEC) in September 2011, which were based at Bobo Dioulasso and operated by the Escadrille de Chasse (Fighter Squadron). They were used against militants in the joint French, Malian and Burkinabé Operation Panga in March

and April 2017, and were also used in anger against militant bases near Pama and Gayeri on September 15, 2018.

The second African nation to fly the Super Tucano was Angola. Six (serial numbers R-701 to R-706) were ordered in March 2012 and the first was handed over in Brazil on January 31, 2013. The aircraft were officially accepted into service on July 12. The Mauritanian Islamic Air Force officially received three aircraft on October 19, 2014, during a ceremony at São Paulo in Brazil. On June 17, 2015, Embraer announced the sale of six Super Tucanos to the Malian Air Force, but the deal was later reduced by two due to financial issues. All four were inducted into service at Air Base 101, adjacent to Bamako International Airport, in July 2018. One was lost in a fatal crash on April 7, 2020.

Two days after the Malian order was announced, it was reported that Ghana had ordered five Super Tucanos;

delivery of the aircraft has not been reported. An earlier order by Senegal for three was also never finalised, with four KAI KT-1Ss being received instead. Brazil also offered to provide Mozambique with financial assistance to acquire three Super Tucanos in 2014, but the offer was rescinded two years later.

Indonesia was the first Asian country to buy the Super Tucano, ordering eight in November 2010. The first four were handed over in Brazil on August 6, 2012, and arrived in Indonesia on September 1, entering service with 21 Skwadron Udara at Abdul Saleh Air Base on East Java. The second batch of four was delivered in September 2014, by when a second order for an additional eight had been placed. These arrived in Indonesia in November 2015 and February 2016.

The Philippines selected the Super Tucano in June 2017

EMB-314 Super Tucano

Length	11.38m (37ft 4in)
Wingspan	11.14m (36ft 6in)
Height	3.97m (13ft)
Empty weight	3,200kg (7,054lb)
Max take-off weight	5,400kg (11,904lb)
Max rate of climb at sea level	988m/min (3,241ft/min)
Max speed at 20,000ft	301kts
Max cruising speed at 20,000ft	286kts
Service ceiling	35,000ft
Max range at 30,000ft	845nm with max fuel and 30-minute reserve
Max external load	1,550kg (3,417lb)
Engine	One Pratt & Whitney Canada PT6A-68/3 turboprop, rated at 1,600shp turning a five-blade Hartzell variable-pitch propeller

Source: Embraer

LEFT • *Chile received 12 Super Tucanos from December 2009 – including this pair of aircraft – to replace Cessna A-37B Dragonflies and form part of the ENAER/CASA 101 fleet. They were augmented by a further six from 2018 and another four in 2020* CEES-JAN VAN DER ENDE

to replace Rockwell OV-10 Broncos, which were heavily involved in the fight against so-called Islamic State (ISIS) affiliated insurgents on the island of Mindanao. An order for six aircraft was signed later that year, with the first four arriving at Clark Air Base on September 19, 2020, and the last two by October 2. They were assigned to the 15th Strike Wing.

American Production

The most unusual purchaser of the Super Tucano was the American private security company Blackwater, which acquired one unarmed aircraft (N314TG) in February 2008 through its subsidiary EP Aviation of McLean, Virginia. It later passed to Tactical Air Support of Reno, Nevada. The aircraft was evaluated by the US Navy as 'BuNo 163056', with the US Mission Design Series designation A-29B (as per the Brazilian Air Force) officially being allocated to the aircraft in August 2008.

It was later armed and equipped with a L-3 Wescam MX-15 electro-optical/infrared sensor and participated in the US Navy's Imminent Fury programme, which sought to acquire systems for anti-irregular warfare. Phase two of Imminent Fury would have been a six-month deployment by four aircraft to Afghanistan, but it was superseded in late 2010 by Combat Dragon II supported by US Central Command. The second phase of Combat Dragon II aimed to test light turboprop attack aircraft in actual combat conditions but was cancelled before it could take place.

US Air Force interest in such aircraft crystalised as the Light Attack/Armed Reconnaissance (LAAR) programme launched in July 2009. Under LAAR the US Air Force sought 100 aircraft to enter service from 2013, but the service's plans to acquire light turboprop strike and reconnaissance aircraft quickly became subject

BELOW • *An A-29B lifts off a dirt strip loaded with four Mk82 general-purpose bombs.* EMBRAER

RIGHT • *The 81st Fighter Squadron of the US Air Force, once based at Moody Air Force Base in Georgia, trained all the pilots for the Afghan Air Force's A-29B fleet. This aircraft is the third assembled by Sierra Nevada Corporation at Jacksonville, Florida.*
US AIR FORCE

to competing requirements and controversy. LAAR was effectively subsumed into the Light Air Support (LAS) project, which sought 20 aircraft for supply to the Afghan Air Force, plus others for the US Air Force for training. The leading contenders for the requirement were the Super Tucano and the AT-6, an armed variant of the T-6 Texan II basic trainer developed by Hawker Beechcraft (later Textron). Embraer teamed with SNC for the competition to provide a US face, with any Super Tucanos ordered to be assembled at Jacksonville in Florida.

Two Super Tucanos were evaluated by the US Air Force at Kirtland Air Force Base in New Mexico between January 25 to 28, 2011, under the Light Air Support System Demonstration. The programme became controversial in November 2011 when the AT-6B was excluded from the selection process, resulting in SNC being awarded a contract on December 22 for 20 A-29Bs for the Afghan Air Force. Work halted in January 2012 after Hawker Beechcraft went to the courts to overturn the deal, and the contract was cancelled on February 28. A new request for proposals was launched on May 4, with SNC again winning the contract on February 27, 2013. The first US Super Tucano (13-2001) assembled at Jacksonville was unveiled on September 25, 2014.

The 81st Fighter Squadron was reactivated under the 14th Flying Training Wing at Moody Air Force Base in Georgia on January 15, 2015, tasked with training 30 Afghan pilots and 90 maintenance personnel on the aircraft. The first four Super Tucanos were delivered to Hamid Karzai International Airport in Afghanistan exactly one year later and the Afghan Air Force began flying combat missions with the aircraft on April 15, 2016. All 20 aircraft in the initial contract had been assembled by the end of July 2016, but an additional order for six was placed by October 2017. By then, 12 Super Tucanos had been delivered to Afghanistan, seven were at Moody and one had been lost in March 2017 in a training accident.

The first of the additional six was delivered on April 24, 2018, and all had been built by September 2020. By then, 18 were in Afghanistan, although a second was written-off on July 9. Afghanistan was overrun by the Taliban in August 2021, following the withdrawal of NATO forces. It is understood that two aircraft then remained at

Moody, but the status of the fleet in Afghanistan is unknown although most, if not all, are likely to be out of service.

In addition to supplying Super Tucanos to Afghanistan, US Air Force interest in light attack aircraft continued under the Capability Assessment of Non-Developmental Light Attack Platforms – unofficially known as OA-X. In late July and into August 2017 four light attack aircraft – including the Super Tucano and AT-6 – were evaluated at Holloman Air Force Base in New Mexico during the Light Attack Experiment (LAE) but plans for a real-world combat demonstration (Combat Dragon III) in February 2018 were abandoned. A second phase of tests began in May 2018 however, but flying activity ended after a Super Tucano crashed over the White Sands Missile Range on June 22, 2018. Both the Super Tucano and AT-6 were declared to be Tier 1 candidates for the role, meeting the requirements of the envisaged mission.

On October 25, 2019, it was announced that two or three A-29Bs and AT-6Bs would be acquired to continue the LAE trials. By the time a contract for two Super Tucanos had been placed in early March 2020 (with a third soon added), interest in LAE had waned. The emphasis had moved on to the US Special Operation Command's (USSOCOM) requirement for an Armed Overwatch aircraft to provide special forces with close air support, precision strike and ISR capability. A total of 75 aircraft was sought. Prototype demonstration contracts were issued to five companies on May 14, 2021, but the

Super Tucano was not one of them.

The second of the three A-29Bs for USSOCOM was delivered to SNC's modification facility on February 23, 2021, joining the first that was already there. All three will be operated by the 6th Special Operations Squadron at Duke Field in Florida to develop an instructor pilot programme for the Combat Aviation Advisory mission to train personnel from partner nations.

SNC has also built A-29Bs for delivery to other customers under the foreign military sales programme. The first was the Lebanese Air Force, which ordered six aircraft on October 30, 2015, equipped with FLIR Systems Brite Star DP electro-optical sensors, and ALE-47 countermeasures dispenser and AAR-60(V)2 missile launch detection systems, in a deal worth US$172.5m. Crew training began at Moody on March 22, 2017, and the first two were delivered to Beirut that October. The final four were ferried to Hamat Air Base in Lebanon in late May 2018.

Nigeria's interest in the Super Tucano began in 2015, but a letter of offer and acceptance was only signed in early 2018. On November 28, 2018, a deal worth US$329m was announced, covering 12 A-29Bs and support, with six of the aircraft to be equipped with FLIR Systems AAQ-22F Brite Star multi-spectral sensor. The aircraft were ordered to counter Boko Haram militants, as well as illicit trafficking within Nigeria and the Gulf of Guinea. The first Nigerian aircraft flew on April 17, 2020, and deliveries to Kainji Air Base, home of 407 Air Combat Training Group, began in July 2021. The aircraft was inducted into Nigerian service on August 31.

SUBSCRIBE AND SAVE

The Global Airline Scene

Published monthly, Airliner World is dedicated to bringing its readers the latest developments. It has a worldwide following comprising both industry readers and commercial aviation enthusiasts. For up-to-the-minute news and features on new leases, deliveries, technology, key industry personnel and airport developments from the airline scene; make Airliner World your magazine of choice!

shop.keypublishing.com/awsubs

GREAT SUBSCRIPTION OFFERS FROM

KEY
Publishing

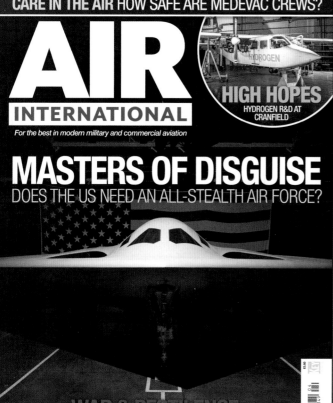

CARE IN THE AIR HOW SAFE ARE MEDEVAC CREWS?

AIR INTERNATIONAL
For the best in modern military and commercial aviation

HIGH HOPES
HYDROGEN R&D AT CRANFIELD

MASTERS OF DISGUISE
DOES THE US NEED AN ALL-STEALTH AIR FORCE?

WAR & PESTILENCE
THE SPARE PARTS MARKET FIGHTS BACK

FRENCH REVOLUTION PILOT TRAINING TRANSFORMED

EXCLUSIVE *INSIDE FINAL BOEING 747 DELIVERY*

AVIATION NEWS
KEY.AERØ THE PAST, PRESENT AND FUTURE OF FLIGHT

ZELENSKYY'S SWING-ROLE SOLUTION?

AFTER THE WALL CAME DOWN
Peek behind the Iron Curtain at East Germany's dying days

Could surplus F-16s take fight to Russia?

PLUS! F-16V Block 70/72 update

POSEIDON PROFILED
Operator-by-operator look at maritime patrol powerhouse

QANTAS
DETAILED: Aussie flag carrier's future fleet

PLUS
• BOEING/NASA BRACED TRUSS PROTOTYPE
• DUXFORD AIRSHOW PREVIEWS
• SIXTIES SYWELL
• REGISTER REVIEW
• AIR BASE MOVEMENTS

Military - Commercial - Unmanned - Engines - Systems & Technology

Over the years, AIR International has established an unrivalled reputation for authoritative reporting across the full spectrum of aviation subjects. We have correspondents and top aviation writers from around the world, offering exciting news, features and stunning photography in each monthly issue.

shop.keypublishing.com/aisubs

The Past, Present and Future of Flight

As Britain's longest established monthly aviation journal, Aviation News is renowned for providing the best coverage of every branch of aviation. With in-depth features, plus first-hand accounts from pilots putting you in the cockpit. Covering both modern military and civil aircraft, as well as classic types, it features subjects from World War Two, through the Cold War years to present day.

shop.keypublishing.com/ansubs

VISIT KEY.AERØ
your online home for aviation

Order direct or subscribe at:
shop.keypublishing.com

Or call UK **01780 480404**
Overseas **+44 1780 480404**
Lines open 9.00-5.30, Monday-Friday

176/23

Commercial Herc

Lockheed Martin is leveraging two decades of the military C-130J's operational service in the LM-100J, currently undergoing flight testing, as Mark Broadbent reports.

Icon is a word that has become much overused in recent years, but it is certainly appropriate when talking about the C-130.

More than 2,600 examples of this enduring workhorse aircraft have now been produced. The type has flown in all parts of the world, from deserts to ice caps, and different variants have flown missions varying from strategic transport and tactical airlift to electronic warfare, disaster response and coastal patrol. The C-130 is arguably the ultimate multipurpose aircraft.

Although C-130s are mainly used by the military, the type is also used in the commercial aviation sector. The L-100 was developed by Lockheed in the early 1960s as a commercial variant of the first-generation C-130. The company produced more than 100 examples at its Marietta, Georgia, facility from 1964 to 1992.

The L-100 has added to the C-130's multipurpose credentials by undertaking a range of specialist missions, from oversize cargo transport work to participating in famine relief efforts in Africa and spraying oil spill dispersant after the Exxon Valdez disaster. More than 30 L-100s remain in service.

A new civil C-130, the Lockheed Martin LM-100J, first flew on May 25, 2017, and is currently in service with one operator.

Testing Work

Two aircraft participated in the LM-100J flight testing programme. The first to fly was N5103D (c/n 5818), the aircraft with the distinctive, blue-painted tail and rear fuselage, which appeared at the 2017 Paris Air Show less than a month after completing its maiden flight from Marietta on May 25. This aircraft was primarily used for avionics testing. The second aircraft, N5105A (c/n 5814), flew on October 11, 2017, and was instrumented for handling and performance testing and some avionics trials.

At the time, Marilou Franklin, certification director of the LM-100J programme at Lockheed Martin, told the author: "In the last year, we've completed almost 5,000 test points and the integration of our development aircraft. We've completed our first TIA, or Type Inspection Authorisation, where we're at a level of maturity where we provided sufficient data to

BELOW • *The first Lockheed Martin LM-100J to fly in May 2017 was N5103D (c/n 5818), which was used for most of the avionics testing.* LOCKHEED MARTIN/TODD MCQUEEN

ABOVE • *An LM-100J prior to cargo loading.* LOCKHEED MARTIN/ MANDIE HARWELL

prove [the aircraft is] ready to go fly for accreditation with the FAA."

It is important to emphasise the LM-100J is a type certificate update of the Lockheed Martin Model L-382J, aka the C-130J.

Lockheed Martin submitted a Program Notification Letter to the FAA for a type design update for the aircraft on January 21, 2014, to produce a civil variant and market it as the LM-100J.

Franklin explained: "We have broken up the type design update for the aircraft into six packages for the FAA. Right now, we're in the third of the six packages and the fourth package is with the FAA; we're getting ready to start flying that. We are well into maturity in the test programme."

Wayne Roberts, the LM-100J Chief Test Pilot, said the first three TIA packages related to handling qualities and performance. At the time of the author's interview, Lockheed Martin was preparing to finish the final assessments of take-off and landing performance with gross weights. Testing of the avionics and the aircraft's carbon brakes was also due for completion shortly thereafter.

Features and Performance

The LM-100J is designed for a range of civil roles, such as transporting bulk and outsize cargo, supporting logistics operations for oil and gas exploration and mining, conducting aerial firefighting and cargo drops, operating medevac/air ambulance and passenger flights, and carrying out humanitarian relief operations and aerial spraying.

The LM-100J is designed to operate into austere locations with short, unprepared strips without ground support equipment and with minimal material handling equipment, with rapid loading and unloading at truck-bed height. The aircraft can carry a 50,000lb (22,679kg) payload and transport outsize cargo. Its cargo floor measures 55 x 10ft (16.7 x 3m) and is 9ft (2.7m) high, and features tie-downs and provisions for roller racks to take ramp-loaded cargo on a standard 463L pallet.

According to Lockheed Martin, compared to its L-100 predecessor the LM-100J can carry one-third more payload, have at least 20% greater range and fly at speeds 10% faster than the L-100. In its promotional literature for the aircraft, the company says an L-100 with a normal gross take-off weight of 155,000lb (70,306kg) and a 35,000lb (15,875kg) payload cruises at 18,000ft at a speed of 280kts. The manufacturer says an LM-100J with the same 35,000lb payload will, by contrast, have a gross take-off weight of 164,000lb (74,389kg), reach a cruising altitude of 28,000ft in less time than it took the L-100 crew to reach 18,000ft, and fly faster at 310kts.

Unsurprisingly, the LM-100J has many similarities to the C-130J. Internally, the aircraft features an enhanced service life centre wing box, enhanced icing protection, and reliability and maintainability improvements that are a part of the basic C-130J design.

The LM-100J is powered by the same Rolls-Royce AE2100D3 turboprops equipped with full authority digital engine control and all-composite Dowty Aerospace R391 six-blade propellers. The engines, each rated at approximately 4,637shp (3,457kW) provide around 150shp (111kW) more power than the legacy Allison T56 engines on the L-100 and comply with FAA Stage IV standards on aircraft noise. The AE2100D3s also have the same automatic engine thrust control system as on the C-130J to adjust automatically for asymmetric thrust conditions if one engine loses power.

As with the military C-130J, the LM-100J is equipped with advanced avionics to fly all-weather missions and at night. It has a glass cockpit with head-up displays and four head-down displays. Colour weather and ground-mapping radar data is presented, and there is a digital autopilot/flight director that can take the aircraft down to Category II minimums (a 100ft decision height for landing with 1,200ft/365m visibility). Franklin said the LM-100J can be flown by operators with a crew of two, should they choose to.

Roberts said the avionics aboard improve the flying experience for crews: "It's always been manoeuvrable for short-field work and in difficult terrain. With just two pilots, the aircraft performs its missions more accurately than it did with five crewmembers on the legacy aircraft."

A further example of how the LM-100J has benefited from the C-130J is the landing gear. Boltless wheels and carbon brakes have been introduced as a retrofit for the C-130J in recent years to improve capability in

ABOVE • LOCKHEED MARTIN/ TODD MCQUEEN

rough-field terrain and provide a longer lifespan (allowing for 2,000 landings per overhaul, up from 250 landings per overhaul previously), thereby creating a maintenance benefit. The upgraded wheels, provided by supplier UTC Aerospace Systems, now Collins Aerospace, to more than 600 C-130Js worldwide, are part of the LM-100J's design and Roberts rates the new gear as "a big improvement" on the L-100.

With the LM-100J designed for commercial operations, inevitably some military-specific hardware and systems on the C-130J have been eliminated to save weight and simplify maintenance requirements. Items that have been removed or disabled include defensive aids, secure communications, racks and wiring for electronic warfare equipment and litter liquid stanchions for casualty evacuation.

The gaseous oxygen tank used on the C-130J for emergencies and its associated ground servicing equipment has been replaced by a simpler gaseous oxygen system with two walk-around oxygen bottles. The C-130J's low-voltage formation lights and station keeping equipment (necessary on the C-130J for formation airdrops) are not installed, and the air deflectors mounted ahead of the doors are deactivated.

However, Roberts pointed out: "From an avionics standpoint, the LM-100J has a mostly common configuration with its C-130J military counterpart. Some military capabilities have been retained, as they support civilian mission requirements, including airdrop. As it is produced, the LM-100J and its avionics are primarily focused on supporting commercial missions as approved by the FAA."

The Benefits of Digital Architecture

The close link with the C-130J is manifested in the LM-100J in other ways. With the C-130J having been in service for over 20 years and with a large operator base spanning over 20 countries, Franklin noted: "There's been an opportunity to bed out any of the problems and issues with reliability on the operational side of things. That's a good platform for the new commercial operators."

One important area where Lockheed Martin feels LM-100J customers will benefit from the C-130J is in the digital architecture. Roberts explained: "When we made the decision in the late 1990s to update the aircraft, we took a step beyond what anyone had done at that point when we digitised it.

"Pretty much everything from wingtip to wingtip, from nose to tail, goes into digital information. The cockpit is completely digitally controlled; there's no hardwire switches in the cockpit. We pioneered a digital computer system throughout the whole aircraft. It receives all this health data and tracks it at a level beyond what anyone had done at that time and I'm not sure anyone has quite caught up yet.

"To give an example, we were the first to put digital circuit breakers on an aircraft; 98% of the circuit breakers on board are digital. It tells the crew if a breaker is popped, and you can isolate [the fault] quickly. That adds to operational reliability and maintainability."

Franklin highlighted the redundancy of the digital architecture (there is a

second mission computer if the first fails) and the MIL-STD-1553 data bus on board provides assurance and security about the information aboard.

The digital architecture also supports a diagnostics system as Franklin explained: "We have a capability to pull anything that's on the system and present it not only to the flight crew but also maintenance on any kind of work that needs to be done. That's a huge advantage in terms of aircraft availability.

"We're going further on the commercial aircraft by incorporating an integrated maintenance system, so when the maintainers look at the diagnostics there's the capability for them to troubleshoot. It provides them with instructions and makes available information as much as possible, so they can maximise their time to the best advantage."

The benefits of this digital capability to an operator's maintenance and operational costs are a fundamental part of the offer to the commercial market Lockheed Martin is making with the LM-100J.

Franklin said: "Commercial operators receive not only a type-certificated aircraft, but also an FAA-approved maintenance programme. We've completed that effort; it was the culmination of two years' work with the FAA and our current legacy fleet operators."

Further strengths are the active C-130J production line and the extensive supply chain that comes from having a global C-130J fleet. With these aircraft having amassed more than three million flying flight hours, Lockheed Martin says LM-100J operators will "have access to an impressive global logistics network, a worldwide support system and insights from known operational and support costs".

Hurricane Response

In September 2017, Hurricane Maria wrought devastation in large parts of the Caribbean. A huge airlift effort was mobilised involving military and civil aircraft. Although it had only flown four months previously and was engaged in flight testing, LM-100J N5103D was one of the aircraft sent in response.

The aircraft deployed from Marietta down to Rafael Hernández Airport in Puerto Rico after Lockheed Martin worked with the FAA to obtain a special permission from the authority for the LM-100J to participate in the relief

LM-100J Characteristics	
Length	112ft 9in (34.3m)
Height	38ft 10in (11.8m)
Wingspan	132ft (40m)
Horizontal tail span	52ft 8in (16m)
Max take-off weight	164,000lb (74,389kg) *
Operating weight empty	81,000lb (36,740kg)
Max zero fuel weight	131,000lb (59,420kg)
Payload	50,000lb (22,679kg) **
Landing distance (with 135,000lb/61,234kg payload)	3,100ft (945m)
Range (with 40,000lb/18,143kg payload)	2,390nm (4,426km)
Max cruise speed	355kts (660km/h)
Engines	Four Rolls-Royce AE 2100D3s each generating 4,637shp (3,457kW) thrust

Data: Lockheed Martin
* Higher maximum take-off and maximum zero fuel weights allowable with wing relieving fuel
** Higher payload allowable with wing relieving fuel

efforts. Two flights were conducted, with the aircraft transporting about 88,000lb (39,916kg) of supplies including water, food, toiletries, and power generators.

Franklin said the FAA providing clearance for the LM-100J to participate in the post-hurricane relief efforts showed the authority's confidence in the platform to be involved in the work, even though it had only been flying for a short while and was still under test. She said the flights were an early showcase of the new aircraft to the aviation world: "It was the aircraft really doing what it was designed to do: be a first responder, provide much-needed supplies and capabilities for people who need it."

What about the LM-100J's market prospects? Tony Frese, vice-president of Business Development, Air Mobility and Maritime Missions at Lockheed Martin, told the author: "Both commercial and government operators have a need for the many missions – humanitarian, oil protection and patrol, firefighting – the L-100 can do, but the LM-100J can do better. There's a market out there for this product across the globe."

To date, Lockheed Martin has one confirmed LM-100J customer: Pallas Aviation based at Fort Worth Alliance Airport, Texas. Pallas ordered five LM-100Js in 2017. To date three have been delivered (N71KM c/n 5854, N96MG c/n 5889 and N67AU c/n 5894, all registered to the Bank of Utah Trustee), and the final two were in the

final stages of production at Marietta as of mid-February, 2023.

Additionally, Lockheed Martin's first LM-100J registered N5103D (c/n 5818) has been sold and delivered to the Algerian Air Force (al-Quwwat al-Jawwiya al-Jaza'iriya) and registered as 7T-WJA. The aircraft arrived in Algeria on January 23, 2022. Based at Boufarik Air Base, the aircraft is assigned to the 2ème Escadre de Transport Tactique et Logistique (2nd Tactical Transport and Logistics Wing).

Letters of intent from two other companies have reportedly been signed: one for ten aircraft signed in 2014 by Shannon-based ASL (which leases seven L-100s through its associate company Safair), and one signed in 2016, again for ten aircraft, from the Brazilian company Bravo.

In support of its C-130J and LM-100J customers, Lockheed Martin built a Hercules Training Center at Marietta which opened in June 2019.

The centre located just steps from the C-130J/LM-100J production line, houses a full FAA-certified Level D simulator, so new LM-100J pilots and crew can be certified within the facility. Re-configurable, Level D simulator technology enables transition between LM-100J, C-130J Block 6 or Block 8.1 training as needed. The centre also supports training needs for military C-130J operators, offers a full spectrum of aircrew training needs including initial qualification, instructor qualification, mission training and refresher courses.

Avanti – Trials and Triumphs

Fast, sleek, and very distinctive, the Piaggio P.180 Avanti is blessed with jet-like performance but the economics of a turboprop. Yet since its first flight in 1986 only around 250 have been produced. David Willis reviews the ups and downs of an Italian classic.

Design studies for what became the Avanti ('forward') began in 1979, with the aim to combine the performance of a jet with the operating economics of a turboprop. Piaggio officially launched the programme in 1982. The chief designer at Piaggio, Alessandro Mazzoni, outlined an aircraft with high-aspect ratio wings, on which were mounted the nacelles for Pratt & Whitney Canada PT6A-66 turboprops in a pusher configuration. The mid-set laminar wing was attached to the fuselage behind the cabin, meaning that the rotating propellers were aligned aft of it, reducing the noise experienced by passengers. In addition to a T-tail, the design had a forward wing mounted

under the nose, with anhedral and landing flaps. The forewing allowed a smaller mainplane to be used, while its greater angle of incidence means it stalls first, automatically lowering the nose.

During 1983 Gates Learjet joined the project to work on the fuselage of what became known as the GP.180. The aerodynamically shaped fuselage, with its greatest depth at the midpoint of the cabin, contributes to the aircraft's lift. Learjet's influence is visible in the large ventral stakes under the rear fuselage and the sharply sloping cockpit windscreen, reminiscent of its own business jet designs. Learjet experienced financial difficulties in the mid-1980s and was forced to cease

work on the GP.180 in January 1986, leaving Piaggio to continue with what then became the P.180 Avanti.

The prototype (I-PJAV) first flew on September 23, 1986, and was followed by the second (I-PJAR) on May 14, 1987. Italian certification was achieved on March 7, 1990, with the initial production Avanti flying on May 30. The US Federal Aviation Administration (FAA) approval was granted on October 2, three days after Robert J Pond of California received the first aircraft delivered as N180BP.

The Avanti was capable of 382kts (707km/h) at 30,000ft (9,144m), making it the fastest turboprop in its category. During 1991 the maximum take-off weight was increased, slightly extending

ABOVE • *The first Avanti was delivered to 'Bob' Pond in the United States in October 1987. The owner of The Palm Springs Air Museum ordered an Avanti II in 2006.* PIAGGIO

RIGHT • *The 'three wing' configuration and pusher propellers make the Avanti one of the most distinctive aircraft ever built. These five aircraft belong to the Italian Air Force, which operates the aircraft as a light transport and for navaid calibration.* PIAGGIO

range. In addition to being standard in new Avantis, the alterations were retrofitted to earlier aircraft.

Customers for the Avanti included Air Enterprise of France, which bought six; Alpi Eagle of Italy, Bulgarian Lucky Flight, Winnair of Germany, and Duncan Aviation of the United States, each of which took two. The Italian Air Force received the first of an initial six it had ordered in 1993.

By early 1995 30 Avantis had been built including the prototypes, but Piaggio was in trouble. The cost of developing the aircraft had drained the company's finances, leaving little to fund production and after-delivery support. In November 1994 the company was placed into administration and ended production of the Avanti.

Rebirth

In November 1998 the Turkish state holding company Tushav acquired a 51% stake in Piaggio, while 44% went to the Italian investment group Aero Trust led by José Di Mase and Piero Ferrari. The company was renamed Piaggio Aero Industries. Aero Trust increased its share to 60% in June 1999. The new owners reassessed the Avanti programme before relaunching production. It would go on to build a further 76 examples of the original variant.

Between 2002 and 2004 studies were undertaken on how to improve the basic design. The three main changes pursued were to increase maximum take-off weight from 5,239kg to 5,511kg

(11,550lb to 12,150lb), give the aircraft a cruising speed of 400kts (740km/h) at 30,000ft (9,144m) – the original target for the design – and introduce a new integrated avionics suite. The additional weight required the landing gear to be strengthened, while the power provided by the PT6A was increased by between eight and 13% in cruise and climb. The Rockwell Collins ProLine 21 suite with three displays was installed in the cockpit.

Known as the Avanti II, the revised variant was certified by the European Aviation Safety Agency (EASA) on October 21, 2005, the same month the 100th example of the earlier version (renamed the Avanti I) was handed over. The first delivery of an Avanti II, to a Swiss customer, occurred in January 2006. Piaggio would go on to deliver around 130 of the model, handing over 30 at its peak in 2008. During October that year Tata of India acquired an approximately one-third share in Piaggio. Three years earlier, in April 2005, an Abu Dhabi government investment fund, the Mubadala Development Company, had secured a 35% stake.

Avantair

The largest operator of Avantis was the US fractional ownership company Avantair, based at Clearwater International Airport in Florida. Established in 2003, ten years later it had 56 of the aircraft. Avantair suspended operations on June 6, 2013,

following an anonymous allegation that it had not tracked time sensitive parts in its fleet. In August 2013 creditors petitioned a bankruptcy court to liquidate the company, after an inspection by the FAA revealed that many of its Avantis were unairworthy and revoked the certificates of airworthiness for the whole fleet.

While the state of the aircraft had nothing to do with Piaggio, the prospect of a quarter of the worldwide fleet being removed from service was alarming. The manufacturer had been hard hit by the slump in sales in the light and midsize sectors that occurred in the early 2000s; it delivered only two new Avantis in 2003.

Piaggio sent a factory team to inspect and detail what work was needed to return Avantair's former aircraft to the air. After consent was given by the Avanti's owner, a Piaggio approved service centre fixed the aircraft so that its certificate of airworthiness could be reissued. The initial former Avantair aircraft returned to the air in October 2013.

HammerHead

Mubadala and Tata increased their holdings in Piaggio to 41% and 44.5% in November 2013, after investing €190m in the company to pursue opportunities in the special missions market. The following month it was announced that the focus of the company would be on the defence and aero engine sectors. Mubadala acquired Tata's

interests in Piaggio in May 2014, giving it over 98% of the shares. Just under 2% was retained by Piero Ferrari, but he sold his interest to Mubadala in September 2015. This was 11 months after the name of the company had changed again, to Piaggio Aerospace, with business units covering civil aircraft production, defence, and security, and powerplant manufacture.

The result of the refocussing on defence was the P.1HH HammerHead medium altitude, long endurance, unmanned air vehicle, based on the Avanti airframe, which was developed in conjunction with Leonardo. It was revealed at the Paris Air Show in June 2013 and a proof-of-concept vehicle first flew on August 8 that year at Decimomannu. A representative prototype, with longer wings, joined the flight programme on December 22, 2014. In May 2016 it was lost off Sicily after around 100 hours of flight testing. A second prototype flew in July 2017

and was later joined by two additional HammerHeads in the development programme.

A launch customer for the HammerHead was secured in March 2016, when the United Arab Emirates Air Force ordered eight for delivery in 2017. Interest in the P.1HH was also expressed by Italy, which was involved in the development programme, but this later focussed on the larger, composite P.2HH, with an endurance of up to 30 hours. Although Italy sanctioned development and expressed a desire for ten systems (each with two airframes), the P.2HH acquisition programme was suspended in 2018.

A second military development, the manned Multirole Patrol Aircraft (MPA), was launched in July 2012 when Piaggio teamed with Abu Dhabi Autonomous Systems Investments. Conceived for maritime surveillance and overland reconnaissance, the MPA retained the basic layout of the Avanti. A prototype

was rolled out in November 2015 and flown in May 2016, but work on the programme had been suspended by mid-2017.

New Factory, New Avanti

Piaggio held a ground-breaking ceremony for a new manufacturing site at Villanova d'Albenga Airport on June 15, 2011, part of its plan to concentrate activity there previously undertaken at Finale Ligure and Genova Sestri Ponente. It officially opened on November 7, 2014, and the first P.180 completed there was the seventh EVO, which was delivered to the Al Saif Group of Saudi Arabia in October 2016.

The EVO was a revised version of the Avanti announced on May 18, 2014, at the European Business Aviation Convention and Exhibition at Geneva, Switzerland. It promised to reduce operating costs while enhancing efficiency, range, and the passenger experience. It would also tackle one of the persistent criticisms of the Avanti, its external noise. While the Avanti II was quieter than a Beech King Air on approach, to the casual listener it did not seem so, as it generated a rasping sound that was the source of complaints from those living near airfields frequented by the type.

For the EVO the original four-blade propellers were replaced by a Hartzell unit with five scimitar blades turning at 1,800rpm (down from 2,000rpm), while low-noise exhaust strakes were fitted to the PT6A-66Bs. The nacelles containing the turboprops were also reshaped. According to Piaggio, these alterations

ABOVE • *The P.1HH HammerHead is a medium altitude, long range, unmanned air vehicle developed from the airframe of the Avanti. Originally ordered by the UAE, the programme was delayed by the loss of the first prototype (seen here).* PIAGGIO

LEFT • *The Multirole Patrol Aircraft was aimed at the maritime and overland surveillance markets. Although a prototype was built the project was abandoned.* PIAGGIO

RIGHT • Rockwell Collins ProLine 21 avionics were introduced in the Avanti II. Although the aircraft has dual controls as standard, it can be operated by a single pilot.
PIAGGIO

reduced external noise levels by 68% (5dBA). The new nacelles, a reshaped front wing and the addition of small winglets contributed to a reduction in fuel burn of 3%, translating into an addition 50nm (92km) of range, while also improving climb performance by 3%. For customers needing to travel further, an optional 177kg (390lb) fuel tank could be installed to extend range to 1,720nm (3,185km). Other changes included a Magnaghi-built landing gear with a 40% increase in the number of cycles it could fly before overhaul (although the Dowty unit was fitted to early production EVOs); anti-skid brakes; digital nosewheel steering; and long-life external LED lights. The cabin was refreshed with leather seats designed by Iacobucci HF, upholstery by Poltrona Frau of Turin, LED lighting and an improved air conditioning system, with optional in-flight entertainment and connectivity systems.

Flight tests of the new nacelles and propeller on a 'standard' Avanti started in the second quarter of 2013, followed by the winglets in the fourth. Three EVOs had been ordered by the time it was revealed, but the first major order was announced at the Farnborough air show in mid-July 2014, when the investment firm Bravia Capital Hong Kong signed for ten, with 40 options. This deal later lapsed.

The Avanti Type Certificate was updated by EASA to incorporate the changes incorporated in the EVO on November 14, 2014. The first for a customer was handed over to Superior Air Services of Megara, Greece, on April 20, 2015.

Seeking a Secure Future

With an improved product and a new factory, Piaggio should have been in a strong position. But only two EVOs were handed over in 2015, three the next year and two in 2017, too few to be economically viable. During September 2017 the Chinese consortium PAC Investments was lined up to acquire Piaggio's civil aircraft division. The sale was blocked by the Italian government on national security grounds, leaving Piaggio in financial trouble. On December 21, 2017, a new five-year industrial plan was approved, in which Mubadala cleared the company's debts and invested €255m to complete development of the HammerHead.

The new planned failed, however. Only four EVOs were delivered in

Piaggio P.180 EVO Characteristics

Wingspan	14.34m (47ft)
Length	14.41m (47ft 3in)
Height	3.98m (13ft)
Max take-off weight	5,488kg (12,100lb)
Max landing weight	5,216kg (11,500lb)
Max zero fuel weight	4,445kg (9,800lb)
Operating empty weight	3,561kg (7,850lb)
Useable fuel	418 US gal (1,583lit)
Cruise speed	401kts (743km/h) max cruising speed at FL310
Ceiling	39,400ft (12,010m) max operating altitude
Seating	Up to 11, including one or two pilot(s)
Range	1,370nm (2,537km) at max cruise power with IFR reserves
Engine	Two Pratt & Whitney Canada PT6A-66B flat-rated to 850shp (634kW) each

2018, while in November 2018 the United Arab Emirates cancelled its HammerHead order, leading Mubadala to exit Piaggio. On November 22, Piaggio Aerospace was declared insolvent and sought 'extraordinary administration' to restructure. Vincenzo Nicastro was appointed the firm's administrator in early December to relaunch Piaggio prior to selling it. Only four EVOs were delivered in 2018 and three the next year, while the plans to save the company were formulated.

In December 2019 the Italian minister of defence placed an order for nine EVOs, four for flight inspection and five transports that could be configured for the medical evacuation role. In addition, Piaggio would upgrade the 18 Avantis already in service with the Italian military. The deal was part of efforts

to make the company attractive to a new owner, with the Italian government stating it wanted to avoid Piaggio being broken up.

Piaggio was put up for sale in February 2020; it delivered no aircraft that year and only one the next. In September 2021 the unidentified preferred bidder was requested by the administrator to put forward a binding offer for Piaggio, but failed to do so, resulting in negotiations with other interested parties restarting at the end of the year. Expressions of interest were expected by the end of February 2022, with five companies reportedly going forward. Italy signed for a further six EVOs in May 2022 for delivery within two years, replacing the earlier plan to upgrade the Italian military's Avantis. It gave Piaggio – and any potential new owner – a total backlog of 17 EVOs.

Swiss Success Story

At the time it was launched Pilatus considered that success for the PC-12 could be claimed if the company sold 250 aircraft over ten years. By the end of September 2022, the Swiss manufacturer had delivered over 1,930, with demand showing no sign of abating. David Willis looks at the variants of Switzerland's most successful aviation export.

Up until the early 1990s Pilatus Aircraft of Stans, Switzerland, was best known for its range of basic trainers and the long-running PC-6 utility transport production programme. It had next to no experience of the business aviation market. By 2000 it had become a major player in the sector, thanks to the PC-12.

The PC-12 was created to fulfil Pilatus' desire to create a new utility aircraft that would appeal to a wide range of different operators. It was conceived as a high-performance, pressurised, single turboprop aircraft, with a large cargo door on the port rear of the fuselage through which freight could be loaded, hoping to increase its appeal to both civil and military customers. The company originally planned freighter (PC-12F), passenger (PC-12P), combi, and military variants of the aircraft.

The cabin was designed to be longer than that of the successful Beechcraft 200 King Air family, while its single powerplant meant it would have lower initial purchase and operating costs than the American twin. Up to nine passengers could be carried for FAR Part 23 certification and six in a business configuration, but up to 14 was planned in high-density seating for military operations. Pilatus believed that the design would carve out its own market, but its estimates of exactly how many it would sell were relatively modest. By early 1993 it held 28 orders and options, including four from the Royal Flying Doctor Service

ABOVE • *The Pilatus PC-12 is the most successful aircraft ever built in Switzerland, with nearly 2,000 delivered in three successive generations. The biggest market for the aircraft is the United States, although PC-12/47 N909PP never made it there, as it was eventually delivered to a Finnish operator.* PILATUS AIRCRAFT

RIGHT • *The Spectre can be equipped with a sensor turret under the rear fuselage. This aircraft is the prototype of the variant, which has been produced in three successive generations.* PILATUS AIRCRAFT

of Australia (which became a major customer for the PC-12).

The PC-12 was announced in October 1989 at the National Business Aviation Association (NBAA) Convention in Atlanta, Georgia. By then, work had been under way on the project for some time and assembly of the prototype had already started. The first prototype completed its maiden flight on May 31, 1991, and was followed by the second on May 28, 1993. Early in the flight campaign it was realised that the wingspan needed to be increased to meet some of the promised performance specifications. In addition to lengthening the span, small winglets were added at the tips, a bullet fairing was added where the tailplane joined the fin, and the dorsal fin and ventral strake were enlarged.

The alterations caused some delay to the original programme schedule, resulting in the aircraft receiving its Type Certificate from the Federal Office of Civil Aviation of Switzerland on March 30, 1994. This was followed by the US Federal Aviation Administration (FAA) on July 15.

Into Production and Service

The original production variant was known as the PC-12 and was offered in Standard (nine passenger) and Executive configurations; Pilatus had shelved plans for a dedicated freighter variant and so the 'PC-12P' effectively became the sole version. As later models were introduced the original version became known as the PC-12/41, the designation coming from the aircraft's maximum take-off weight of 4,100kg (9,039lb). It was powered by a Pratt & Whitney Canada PT6A-67B, flat-rated at 1,207shp (900kW) for five minutes and 1,006shp (750kW) for continuous operation. The Bendix/King Gold Crown electronic flight instrument system was fitted as standard and from the outset the PC-12 could be flown by a single pilot; in the third quarter of 1997 the aircraft was approved for commercial single-engine IFR operations. Deliveries began in September 1994 with the first (N312BC c/n 101) going to the Carlson Leasing Corporation in the United States, one of six handed over that year.

Work on a higher maximum weight variant, up to 4,500kg (9,921lb), resulted in the PC-12/45 which became the baseline version in 1997. In addition to aircraft built as such PC-12/41s could

also be upgraded to the new standard. As demand increased production was increased in August 1997 from three a month to four. That year Kelner Airways of Canada became the first scheduled service airline operator to fly the PC-12.

By 1999 a total of 140 PC-12s (plus the two prototypes) had been built, with nearly two-thirds going to customers in the United States. They included 11 for Community Air of California, which became the first in the country to take advantage of new rules from the FAA

to carry fare-paying passengers in a single-engined aircraft in IFR conditions. Alpha Flying's PlaneSense programme, based at Nashua, New Hampshire, became the initial fractional ownership programme to use the single-turboprop aircraft, taking the 20th production example; it would go on to play an important role in the PC-12 story. The 200th sale was announced in October 1999 and production increased from 48 to 60 annually. By then, the aircraft was certified in 12 countries,

ABOVE • *The PC-12 NGX is the current production version and the first powered by the Pratt & Whitney Canada PT6E-67XP. The variant can be identified by its larger cabin windows.*
PILATUS AIRCRAFT

which quickly rose to 20. The PC-12 is currently approved by over 26 aviation authorities.

Paramilitary PC-12s

Work on a special mission variant was begun by Pilatus in 1995 as the Eagle. The second prototype PC-12, HB-FOB, was modified and reflown in the new configuration that October, making its debut at the Dubai Air Show the following month. It was offered for a diverse range of roles, including navaid calibration, aerial survey, airborne communications relay, and medevac. The demonstrator was equipped with a large ventral pannier, necessitating larger strakes under the rear fuselage to maintain directional stability, and lacked the winglets of the commercial variant. A second demonstrator, HB-FOG, equipped with different mission equipment followed in September 1996, while a third Eagle was created in 1999 as an airborne cellphone relay station. The first announced sale of an Eagle was to the Swiss Defence Procurement Agency; in fact, this was the second demonstrator, which was based at Emmen and used to test the FLORAKO air defence radar system.

In 2002 Pilatus introduced the Multi Role Aircraft, which was marketed as the Spectre from the following year. The Spectre did away with the ventral pannier, instead having a retractable sensor turret under the rear fuselage, controlled by an operator's console in the cabin. Exactly what mission

equipment was carried depended on the requirements of the customer, resulting in different configurations, although Spectres retained the standard winglets of the commercial PC-12. The prototype, N146PC, flew in June 2003 and the US Bureau of Immigration and Customs Enforcement (ICE) was identified as the initial customer, eventually acquiring three.

At least three different generations of Spectre have been produced, differing in equipment options, and using different baseline PC-12 variants. In addition to ICE, other customers included the Gendarmeria of Argentina; Bulgarian Air Force; Government of Chad; the Police Department of Phoenix, Arizona; Western Australia Police, and US Bureau of Land Management. The aircraft for last two were equipped with the Utility/Jump Door modification, which allowed people or packages to be air dropped without depressurising the cabin.

The Draco

In October 2005, the US Mission Design Series designation U-28A was given to six PC-12s acquired by Air Force Special Operations Command (AFSOC) on the civil market. The aircraft entered service with the 319th Special Operations Squadron (SOS)/16th Special Operations Wing (SOW) based at

Hurlburt Field, Florida, and were initially flown with N-numbers before adopting US military identities. An additional four entered service in 2007 and the fleet subsequently increased until around 40 PC-12s had been acquired (although not all may have become U-28As). They later served with the 318th and 551st SOS of the 27th SOW based at Cannon AFB, New Mexico, and the 5th, 19th and 34th as well as the 319th SOS at Hurlburt Field.

Very little substantive information has been released on the U-28A. It is known that they were acquired under the Non-Standard Aviation (Light) programme run on behalf of AFSOC by the Big Safari project office. Work on the aircraft was undertaken by the Sierra Nevada Corporation (SNC) at Centennial Airport, Colorado, possibly including the installation of the mission equipment for their intelligence surveillance reconnaissance (ISR) role. The aircraft carried an electro-optical sensor with a co-aligned laser designator and were equipped with an advanced communications suite, including datalinks, although the equipment installed in individual aircraft is understood to differ. The crew of four includes a combat and a tactical systems operator in the cabin and two pilots. The popular name Draco was approved for the U-28A in May 2019.

U-28As served in the conflicts in Afghanistan and Iraq, and the aircraft has also operated in East Africa (one was lost heading back to Camp Lemonnier in Djibouti on February 18, 2012) and in other regions on the continent. The aircraft is due to be replaced in the Armed Overwatch role by the L3Harris Technologies AT-802U Sky Warden.

Military Operators

In addition to the US Air Force, the PC-12 has served with or is still flown by the air forces of Botswana, Bulgaria, Chad, Finland, Ireland, South Africa, and Switzerland. Some of the aircraft delivered were Spectres or were modified to undertake ISR roles, while others serve as light or VIP transports.

The largest fleet was delivered to Afghanistan and operated by the Special Mission Wing until the Taliban gained control of the country. Of the 16 PC-12s delivered, five were reportedly equipped for electronic ISR by SNC. Following the departure of US forces from Afghanistan in August 2021 two of the aircraft were rendered inoperative at Hamid Karzai International Airport in Kabul. Eleven were flown to Temez International Airport in Uzbekistan and three to Bokhtar International in Tajikistan, where they remain under US custodianship awaiting their fate.

Of the other military operators, Finland has the largest fleet, having used six PC-12 NGs (New Generation) from 2010 in the light transport role. From 2020, Ireland acquired four PC-12 NGs. Most of the other nations have single examples of the PC-12.

New Generation

On November 8, 2005, Pilatus announced a further growth in take-off weight of the baseline aircraft to 4,740kg (10,450lb), permitting range to expand by 350nm (648km) or an additional 240kg (529lb) of payload to be carried. The new variant – known as the PC-12/47 – introduced a new, flatter winglet design that enhanced aileron control and improved the aircraft's crosswind handling. Pilatus also refreshed the interior of the PC-12 with new seats and introduced LED cabin lighting, while LEDs also replaced bulbs for exterior navigation lights.

The PC-12/47 became available from January 2006 and was certified by the European Aviation Safety Agency (EASA) on June 23. It was the last version of the initial generation of the PC-12 (alongside the /41 and /45) offered, production of which amounted to 787 aircraft in total, plus the two prototypes. The last example was delivered to Share Plane AG of Switzerland in June 2008.

Pilatus announced the PC-12 NG in October 2006. The New Generation variant replaced the original subtype of the PT6A turboprop with the PT6-67P, flat rated at 1,172shp (862kW) for take-off and 1,000shp (735kW) in the cruise, increasing speed by 13kts (24km/h) while flying at Flight Level 210. The PC-12 NG also addressed one of the criticisms of the aircraft at the time, its somewhat dated cockpit. The Swiss company engaged BMW Group DesignworksUSA to redesign the 'front office' to maximise comfort and efficiency, while also introducing a fully integrated glass cockpit in the form of the Honeywell Primus Apex, with four screens (two primary flight and two multifunctional displays) as standard.

The prototype PC-12 NG (technically designated the PC-12/47E) first flew on October 6, 2006, and participated in avionics and autopilot development trials in North America for the variant. It was followed into the air by the initial production example on August 14, 2007. The PC-12 NG was approved by both EASA and the FAA on March 28, 2008, and Western Aircraft of Boise, Idaho,

ABOVE • A significant percentage of PC-12s are used in the air ambulance role. The most famous operator in the role – with one of the largest fleets – is the Royal Flying Doctor Service of Australia. DAVID WILLIS

RIGHT • Honeywell Primus Apex avionics in the cockpit of the PC-12 NG, with a primary flight display for each pilot and stacked multifunctional displays in the centre. Although every PC-12 has dual controls a single pilot can fly the aircraft. PILATUS AIRCRAFT

Pilatus PC-12 NG Characteristics

Wingspan	16.28m (53ft 5in)
Length	14.40m (47ft 3in)
Height	4.26m (13ft 1in)
Max Take-off Weight	4,740kg (10,449lb)
Max Landing Weight	4,500kg (9,920lb)
Max Zero Fuel Weight	4,100kg (9,038lb)
Operating Empty Weight	3,076kg (6,781lb)
Useable Fuel	402 US gal (1,522lit)
Cruise Speed	285kts max cruising speed
Ceiling	30,000ft (9,145m) max certified altitude
Seating	Up to nine passengers, plus one or two pilot(s)
Range	1,460nm (2,703km) at FL300 with four passengers and IFR reserves
Engine	One Pratt & Whitney Canada PT6A-67P flat-rated to 1,200shp (895kW)

became the first customer to receive the variant on May 27.

Pilatus delivered the 1,200th production PC-12 on August 3, 2013, to Alpha Flying for its PlaneSense fractional ownership programme. By then, the company had become the largest customer for the PC-12, having received 49 (including some to replace earlier aircraft) at the time of the delivery. At the start of 2020, it had 36 PC-12s in its fleet.

From the 2016 model the five-blade Hartzell composite propeller became standard. Along with several aerodynamic improvements it increased cruise speed of the PC-12 NG by a further 5kts. During 2016 a total of 91 PC-12s were delivered, while at least 80 were shipped in each subsequent year up to 2021 (the last year for which data is currently available).

The current production model is the PC-12 NGX, which was announced at

the 2019 NBAA Convention in Las Vegas, Nevada. The PC-12 NGX is powered by the PT6E-67XP, flat rated at 1,100shp (809kW), which also benefits from an electronic propeller and engine control system. The new powerplant propels the PC-12 NGX along at 290kts in the cruise. The aircraft is also equipped with autothrottles to reduce pilot workload and has upgraded Honeywell avionics, while passengers in the cabin look through 10% larger windows in a redesigned interior.

The NGX is unlikely to be the last version of the PC-12 produced. A third of a century after it made its first flight and with over 10 million flight hours logged, the Swiss aircraft continues to be the best-selling single-engine turboprop in its class. The 2,000th example is expected to be delivered at some point during the spring of 2023. Fittingly, it is due to go to PlaneSense.

High-Performer

Riccardo Niccoli profiles the Swiss turboprop – and gains a first-hand experience flying in it.

The Pilatus PC-21 is different from other turboprop trainers in its performance and its advanced training system capabilities. Should the PC-21 be considered an evolution of the earlier PC-9? Absolutely not - it is a completely new design, conceived to produce a new generation training system to train student pilots not only in the basic phase of their syllabus, but in the advanced and lead-in fighter training (LIFT) phases.

Many years ago, an expert aviation engineer told the author: "If you want to understand an aircraft, to know what it has been designed for, to catch its soul, just look at the wing."

The PC-9 wing is straight, thick, with a span of 10.12m (33ft 3in), an area of 16.3m2 (175.5ft2), an aspect ratio of 6.3, and with a maximum take-off weight (MTOW) a typical wing load of 138.1kg/m2 (28.3lb/ft2). In contrast, the PC-21 wing is 13° swept, with winglets, has a laminar airfoil, a span of 9.10m (29ft 11 in), an area of 14.9m2 (160.4ft2), an aspect ratio of 5.1, and the MTOW aerobatic wing load is 208kg/m2 (42.6lb/ft2).

This comparison shows how the PC-21 was designed to be faster and more agile than the PC-9. You can also see this by comparing the engine power of the two aircraft: 950shp (708kW) for the PC-9 against a staggering 1,600shp (1,193kW) for the PC-21. Finally, the PC-21 has a very sleek and aerodynamic form that gives you an impression of speed even on the ground. It is not a

traditional, straight-wing trainer. Pilatus's idea was to create a turboprop that had all the advantages of a light turboprop aircraft coupled with the handling, performance, and feeling of a jet trainer.

Did they succeed? The author was given the opportunity to find out during a two-day immersion in the PC-21 environment at Pilatus's home plant at Stans in Switzerland.

Project Pillars

The author was given briefings on the PC-21 training system, the aircraft equipment, and avionics from Raimund Sauer (a former Luftwaffe F-4 pilot, now Pilatus' regional sales director) and Martin Mendel (a former Luftwaffe Tornado pilot and T-6 instructor at Sheppard Air Force Base, today

ABOVE • *A Schweizer Luftwaffe (Swiss Air Force) PC-21 over the Aletsch Mountain. Note the wing tip form.* SCHWEIZER LUFTWAFFE

RIGHT • *The white fuselage stripe applied to Schweizer Luftwaffe PC-21 aircraft visually exaggerates the elegant aerodynamic form of the PC-21's fuselage.* SCHWEIZER LUFTWAFFE

Pilatus' production test pilot and flight instructor).

The PC-21 was launched in November 1998, and the first prototype, registered HB-HZA, flew for the first time on July 1, 2002. The launch customer was the Republic of Singapore Air Force, which received the first of 19 aircraft in April 2008, followed by the Schweitzer Luftwaffe (Swiss Air Force), which received six in April 2008 and its final two in 2012. Since then, Pilatus has received the following orders.

Operator	Date	Quantity
Armee de l'Air (French Air Force)	January 2017	17
Ejército del Aire y del Espacio (Spanish Air and Space Force)	November 2019	40
Qatar Emiri Air Force	July 2012	24
Royal Australian Air Force	September 2015	49
Royal Jordanian Air Force	Q1 CY2016	12
Royal Saudi Air Force	May 2012	55
UAE Air Force and Air Defence	November 2010	25

The reasons for this success can be easily identified in the quality of the Swiss factory's products and support, many of the air forces listed were already Pilatus customers, but also in the philosophy at the heart of the aircraft.

There are three aspects of the PC-21 that make the type so attractive to an air force: its performance, its low costs and the full training system that comes with the aircraft.

The wing and aerodynamics, coupled with the 1,600shp Pratt & Whitney Canada PT6A-68B turbine and a 92in (2.33m) Hartzell five-blade graphite/titanium propeller, can launch the aircraft to a 337kts (624km/h) maximum cruising speed at 10,000ft (3,048m), and allow a maximum climb rate (sea level) of 4,250ft/min (21.59 m/sec).

What is interesting is that such performance can be attained with a purchase price that Pilatus claims is about 25% that of a LIFT jet, with a 50% less direct operating cost to the nearest jet-powered competitor.

Today, key to reducing training costs is the ability to download training activity from advanced training units to the basic and advanced phases, using modern and efficient aircraft, well-integrated into a ground-based simulation system and an embedded in-flight simulation system. These capabilities are necessary because the fighter pilots of today and tomorrow are now dedicated to managing their weapons systems as well as purely flying their aircraft, and the longest part of a pilot's training today is getting them used to managing all the various modes and capabilities of their flying computers. The PC-21 can be used to perform the basic, advanced and LIFT phases, as well as by navigators and weapons system operators.

The Aircraft

The PC-21, with its 3,100kg (6,834lb) MTOW in aerobatic configuration, is a light aircraft. Its wing houses the fuel tanks (about 1,200lb/544kg in total) and it is equipped with flaps and spoilers (the latter increase the roll rate). The damage-tolerant airframe has been designed for +8/-4 g loads (aerobatic), or for +5/-2.5g at the maximum utility weight (4,250kg/9,370lb), and has a demonstrated, conservative life limit of 15,000 flight hours, based on a fighter aircraft-derived design spectrum (the full-scale fatigue test airframe completed 45,000 simulated flight hours). Other interesting features include the stepped cockpit, with a front canopy that can resist bird strikes at high cruise speeds, the pressurised cabin equipped with an anti-g system and two Martin-Baker Mk-CH16C zero/zero ejection seats. There is an onboard oxygen generation system, a health and usage monitoring system, anti-skid brakes and a pressure refuelling system.

The scheduled maintenance is set only at 150 and 300 hours, and there is no need for depot overhauls. Every part and system on the PC-21 is easily accessible thanks to large service panels, including one on the bottom fuselage that allows the mechanic to stand inside the avionics bay. An advanced support equipment package includes integrated electronic technical publications. A fast turnaround can be carried out by a single mechanic in just 12 minutes.

The Cockpit

Heart of the PC-21 is its glass cockpit, and its embedded simulation capability. The front cockpit is dominated by three large (150 x 200mm/6 x 8in) night-vision goggles (NVG)-compatible active-matrix liquid crystal multifunction displays (MFDs), and a head-up display (HUD). The rear cockpit is pretty much the same, except for an HUD, which is replaced by a HUD repeater.

ABOVE • *A tight formation of two PC-21s over the mountains of Switzerland.* PILATUS

The cockpit layout is like those of the Typhoon, Rafale, and Gripen: Pilatus can customise the avionics symbology according to the customer's needs. The MFDs can display a wide variety of pages. Usually, the primary flight display (PFD, showing all the flight instruments) is selected in the middle, while the moving map display, navigation and tactical display or synthetic radar display can be shown on the left. On the right is the weapons configuration page (simulated), and the engine and fuel data display. For basic training, the two lateral MFDs can be turned off and only the middle PFD left on for the student, while the instructor in the back seat can use all three MFDs to maximise situational awareness.

These systems are all controlled by the Open System Mission Computer (OSMC). Above the two lateral MFDs, there are other instruments, a secondary flight display and an engine monitoring display (these are not driven by the OSMC and provide a back-up in case of failure of the main systems). Above the PFD is the up-front control panel, which allows control of the navigation and communication systems, as well as the weapons delivery.

The navigation/communications suite can be tailored to the customer's needs, but as the PC-21 has civil as well as military certification, it has a complete equipment fit-out, including VHF/UHF radios, emergency locator transmitter, automatic dependent surveillance-broadcast receiver, inertial reference system integrated with a GPS, digital air data computer, two VOR/ILS, distance measuring equipment, a radar altimeter, and a flight management system. Other systems can be integrated, such as a tactical air navigation system, and an autopilot and flight director system.

Flight controls comprise a stick in the middle, and a throttle (called the Power Control Lever or PLC) on the left side flanked by the flap selector. The controls follow the hands-on throttle and stick philosophy and include 15 switches and buttons offering a wide variety of control options, including radar modes and radar target selection, weapons release, boresight missile, chaff, flare, and more. They, as well as the HUD and radar display, can be configured to the needs of the customer, for example replicating the Typhoon, F-16, or F/A-18 controls.

The embedded simulation capability includes the ability to operate synthetic air-to-air and air-to-ground radar representations (simulating the APG-65, APG-68, or other radar systems), real time datalink, simulated stores management and use of simulated weapons for air-to-air and air-to-ground, including onboard synthetic target generation, simulated chaff and flare, and radar warning receiver. The system allows the cockpit configuration to be split to simulate systems failure or data degradation, and includes a mission data recorder with video, audio, and data recording.

Integrated Training System

An Integrated Training System (ITS) is a must in the training sector, as it offers further reductions in training costs. The Pilatus ITS is formed by various

ABOVE • *The PC-21 features two cockpits in a stepped configuration each dominated by three large 6 x 8in multifunction displays.* PILATUS

Pilatus PC-21 Characteristics

Length	11.23m (36ft 11in)
Wingspan	9.11m (29ft 11in)
Height	3.75m (12ft 4in)
Wing area	14.9m² (160.4ft²)
Basic empty weight	2,340kg (5,159lb) depending on configuration
Max take-off weight (aerobatic)	3,100kg (6,834lb)
Max take-off weight (utility)	4,250kg (9,370lb)
Take-off distance (SL, 50ft obstacle)	725m (2,380ft)
Landing distance (SL, 50ft obstacle)	900m (2,953ft)
Max rate of climb (SL)	21.59 m/sec (4,250ft/min)
Max operating speed	370kts (685km/h, Mach 0.72)
Max cruise speed (SL)	323kts (598km/h)
Max cruise speed (10,000ft)	337kts (624km/h)
Design dive speed	420kts (778km/h)
Stall speed (clean)	92kts (170km/h)
Stall speed (gear and full flap)	81kts (150km/h)
G loads (acrobatic)	+8 /-4g
G loads (utility)	+ 5 /-2.5g
Max range	720nm (1,333km)
Max endurance	2.5 hours
Ceiling	38,000ft (certified to 25,000ft)

Data: Pilatus

elements. The ground-based training system includes training documents and aids, computer-based training, personnel training, synthetic training devices, and all studies that take the student from zero to the first flight, and beyond. The hardware is formed by the aircraft systems trainer, the integrated procedure trainer, and the flight training device. The latter is a full simulator with the cockpit housed inside a dome, capable of providing a 320o angle of view (or even more if required).

When preparing for flight training, a student can prepare all their flight plans using the mission planning system, which manages navigation, communication, the radar, weapons, targets, and other data. All the information selected is used by the system to prepare routes and scenarios.

Next all the mission data is transferred into a removable memory module, also simply called a brick, a 64GB cassette that can be inserted in the aircraft, or in the simulator mission data recorder (MDR). During the mission (real or simulated), from the avionics switch-on to the switch-off, the MDR records all the data and parameters, including full colour images from the HUD and the MFDs.

Post-mission, the student takes the brick from the aircraft and goes to the debriefing phase, where – thanks to the mission debriefing system (MDS) – they, together with their instructor, can review all the phases of the flight. They use three different screens: one dedicated to the HUD, another to a 3D graphical representation of the mission and a third dedicated to the cockpit MFDs. The MDR records all the parameters, so it can also display data from pages

that were not selected by the pilots during the flight. The MDS runs on a commercial off-the-shelf high-capacity computer and can display a maximum of four sorties together.

During the mission, the instructor (who can fly in either the front or aft cockpit, according to the training needs) is able to isolate the two cockpits to access the aircraft's library and sensor data and make modifications without the students knowing. This means the instructor can modify the mission, introduce failures, or change parameters, and even the flight parameters of other synthetic enemy aircraft involved in the mission.

Simulation

In air-to-air training missions, the MFDs can show various missile modes (generic short-range infrared-guided, or generic medium range radar-guided missiles) and gun modes in lead-computed optical sight or continuously computed optical sight, with sound tones in the headset if needed. When flying air-to-air against another PC-21, the datalink allows each aircraft to see the other in the virtual radar system, in

the same way that it would if the pilots had a real radar.

In air-to-ground training activity, the simulation makes it possible to fly against pre-designated ground targets releasing virtual bombs with continuously computed release point or continuously computed impact point (CCIP) techniques. It's possible to release by dive, toss or with CCIP for unguided rockets. The synthetic air-to-ground capability of the radar is included.

In both air-to-air and air-to-ground roles, the instructor can select the on-board scoring system page on an MFD, which provides real-time (and post-flight) results in terms of the success of the weapons used against the targets engaged during the mission. Air-to-ground scoring also provides a virtual and range-typical 'o'clock score' with distance in feet from the desire mean point of impact. The scoring meticulously records all relevant aircraft parameters during the moment of weapon release, like speed, dive-angle, ground speed and range to the target, giving the instructor the

opportunity for immediate analysis and feedback to the student.

The ground-based training system and the aircraft are complemented by an integrated logistic support system, which grants a very high level of efficiency of the fleet.

Conclusions

Immersion in the PC-21 world showed the author a surprising aircraft. It goes beyond the traditional basic turboprop trainer concept, and clearly enters the field of advanced trainers in terms of performance and avionics. This author considers it an aircraft with two applications: one is that of a basic turboprop trainer, easy to handle, and with comfortable speeds in many critical parts of the flight envelope, especially in the landing phase, that are suitable even for young pilots with very limited flying experience. The second is a high-performance aircraft that cruises

at relatively high speeds and boasts an avionics suite worthy of the best advanced jet trainers. The embedded simulation capability, and the possibility of in-depth debriefings offered by the system, is remarkable. The best testimonial is that the Schweitzer Luftwaffe passes PC-21 students directly onto the F/A-18C Hornet as a standard pipeline.

That said, the PC-21 cannot completely replicate an advanced jet trainer as its speeds and performances at altitudes above 15,000ft (4,572m) to 25,000ft (7,620m) cannot match those of its LIFT competitors, such as the Leonardo M-346, the KAI T-50 or the BAE Systems Hawk.

Consequently, some PC-21 operators, such as Singapore, Saudi Arabia, and the UAE, still operate advanced jet trainers for LIFT training. Using a PC-21 for an entire LIFT phase could mean students have to attend a longer training phase at an operational conversion unit

than if a LIFT jet was also used. True evaluation of the two different systems can only be made by each air force.

Some may decide on the importance of a LIFT to provide high speeds, altitudes, and energy, to get the students used to the performance of the frontline jets. Others may consider it a waste of money to acquire and operate a LIFT jet, when you can carry out nearly all the military training on the PC-21 training system. According to Pilatus, the PC-21 flying cost per hour is about 40 times cheaper than that of a modern fighter.

Of course, any decision on this subject depends on the traditions and attitudes of the air forces' decision makers.

In any case, Pilatus seems to be leading the field – as production at Stans goes on, and an increasing number of new potential customers show their interest in this little Swiss jewel.

ABOVE • *The PC-21 has a roll rate of 200° per second.* SCHWEIZER LUFTWAFFE

RIGHT • *Coloured tips of the 92in Hartzell graphite/titanium propellers seen against a snowy backdrop.* SCHWEIZER LUFTWAFFE

Airborne in the PC-21

The author was given the opportunity to try the PC-21 flight training device for a good hour to familiarise himself with the cockpit, its controls and the aircraft's flight performance.

Production test pilot and flight instructor Martin Mendel allowed the author to perform some standard manoeuvres, while Martin demonstrated the embedded simulation in air-to-air and air-to-ground modes. Though a flight simulator cannot exactly render a real flight, the author was able to appreciate that at low speeds the PC-21 remains an easy aircraft to fly. An approach can be set at about 105-110kts, and the final, flare and touchdown phases can be managed by the pilot as in a normal turboprop or propeller trainer of far lower performance and power.

Day two of the author's visit started at 08:00hrs with the briefing for the first flight, a single-ship mission to demonstrate the PC-21's flight qualities, navigation, and embedded simulation in the air-to-ground mode in the third PC-21 built HB-HZC (c/n 101).

The author found the rear cockpit comfortable with excellent visibility thanks to the stepped tandem seats.

Once all the usual procedures to secure oneself to the seat and to the survival systems (belts, leg strains, survival pack, anti-g, oxygen mask and radio jack plugs) are completed, it was time to close the canopy. Martin reminded the author to lower his helmet visor. The PC-21's front canopy features a miniature detonating cord that will shatter it in the case of an ejection. This system is necessary because the front part of the canopy is built to resist high-speed bird strikes and cannot be safely broken by the ejection seat alone. The start-up procedure is quite simple and quick. Power on, then push the start button and, above 13% Ng (the RPM) move the throttle to idle position.

Martin taxied the aircraft to take-off from runway 25, lined-up on the 6,600ft (2,000m) runway, take-off clearance was received from the tower when Martin gently increased the engine's power and released the brakes. The thrust was strong, but easily controllable, thanks to some special features designed by Pilatus to make the PC-21 handling like that of a jet. From zero to

80kts, the Power Management System (PMS) delivers 1,080shp. To compensate for the high torque forces, the engine is installed with a 2° angle to the right of the centreline, and the tail features an auto yaw compensation called TAD (Trim Aid Device). To keep the aircraft on the runway centreline during the take-off run requires only a few touches of the right pedal, and at 92kts, after some 13 seconds, with a gentle pull of the stick, the aircraft is in the air.

With the landing gear and take-off flaps retracted the PC-21 rapidly gained speed. Above 200kts, the engine delivers all its 1,600shp, and with even less than 100% torque, the aircraft easily reached a cruise speed of 270kts, with a fuel flow of 840lb/hour. The feeling is different from other propeller aircraft, as we fly smoothly and quietly, without noise or vibrations.

The first part of the flight was a navigation route around some big mountains in the Alps, over Engelberg, near the Titlis peak (10,697ft/3,239m), then over the Gadmental valley, passing close to the Wetterhorn, past the Eiger's north face, the Jungfraujoch (11,468ft/3,475m) and over the Aletsch Glacier, the biggest in the Alps. At that altitude, with a 100% power setting, the fuel flow was about 750lb/hour.

Passing south of the Fiescherhorn, Martin dived the aircraft at 300kts down into the 'S' canyon of the Unterer Grindelwald Glacier with strong southerly tail winds, which showed the aircraft's good handing and stability, thanks to the relatively high wing load.

The navigation systems, displayed on the left MFD, gave a clear representation of the ground

map, the waypoints, and the other necessary information.

Martin then flew the aircraft into an area of airspace over Lake Lucerne. At around 10,000ft, Martin demonstrated stalls and spins. With the aircraft in clean configuration, the stall occurred at about 90kts, while the spin was less conventional and is slightly harsher. Martin performed four stable spins, losing some 500ft per turn, but the recovery was simple, and followed the rules valid for all straight-wing propeller aircraft: to stop the spin, reduce power to idle, apply opposite rudder and centre the stick.

Martin then demonstrated some basic aerobatics. First a loop, which can be started at any speed above 200kts, but 250kts is more comfortable pulling 3.5 to 4 g, and with limited use of the rudder, only on top of the loop.

Then Martin demonstrated a roll that allowed the author to experience the PC-21's high roll rate of 200°/sec made possible by the roll spoilers located on the wing, which operate in conjunction with the normal, but hydraulically boosted, ailerons. Generally, the author found the sequence of rolls quite comfortable; the stick was precise and soft, the perfect compromise at all speeds considering that to save weight, the flight controls maintain the traditional cable system, the ailerons are hydraulically assisted, and the roll spoilers hydraulically powered.

The final phase of the flight demonstrated the embedded simulation capability in the air-to-ground field, including a synthetic air-to-ground radar mode. The author was given the opportunity to see how the avionics system simulates the delivery of bombs with a level profile, and with 30° dive profile (using the CCIP mode), then the launch of unguided rockets, and finally a strafing run.

The author rated the representations in the HUD, and the ability to switch the right MFD to the instructor page and look in real time at the results of the firings, as very good. In addition to this virtual weapon release capability, the PC-21 has five underwing hardpoints which can carry up to 2,535lb (1,150kg), such as two 250lit ferry tanks each weighing 450lb.

For landing, Martin lowered the flaps, and when below 180kts, the

landing gear, with the engine set as required to maintain the correct position of the speed indicator in the HUD.

On final approach, Martin selected flaps to the 34° land position and the speed decreased gently until touchdown at 87kts, and with a normal use of the brakes the aircraft slowed down rapidly for an easy exit from the runway. At the end of the 60-minute flight the aircraft had 600lb of fuel remaining.

A second flight demonstrated the embedded simulation for air-to-air training. Using the PC-21's datalink system to exchange the data between two aircraft, allows the system to represent the signals as contacts on a radar screen, shown on one of the MFDs.

Once in the assigned airspace, operating between 15,000-25,000ft (4,545-7,575m), the two PC-21s started with a series of turns and lazy eights in close formation to demonstrate the behaviour of the aircraft.

During beyond visual range engagements, the datalink worked perfectly, and gave the position of the enemy aircraft on the radar screen, and on the moving map, with a red triangle.

The first head-on run involved target engagement using the radar's scan mode and a Fox 3 missile (typically a radar-guided missile in the AMRAAM class) launched within its maximum range resulting in a kill on the enemy aircraft. In the second run, the radar is in track-while-scan mode and the missile fired outside its range resulting in another kill on the enemy aircraft.

A second phase was dedicated to demonstrating within visual range (WVR) air combat, against a manoeuvring target at a maximum of 3g and 150kts minimum speed.

The first two engagements involved launch of a Fox 2 missile (typically an infrared-guided weapon, such as the AIM-9L Sidewinder) while both aircraft were flying low and high yo-yos. The system replicates the missile launch procedures very well, including the acoustic tone in the headset. A third run was dedicated to air-to-air gunnery.

On recovery to Buochs after a 45-minute sortie, the aircraft had 750lb of fuel remaining in the wing tanks.

For Business and Pleasure

The Piper PA-46 Malibu family reached its zenith when its airframe was mated with a powerful turboprop. David Willis details the development of the PA-46-500TP Malibu Meridian family, the M500 and the flagship M600.

The M500 is the mid-range member of Piper's current 'M-Class' of single-engine, pressurised, light business aircraft, falling between the piston-engined M350 and the faster turboprop M600 in its product range. All three aircraft can trace their roots back to the original Piper PA-46 Malibu. The Malibu was conceived in 1977 as part of Piper Aircraft's aggressive plan to increase its share of the general aviation market from 26% to 50%. To achieve this goal, the company needed a new product, and its planners had their eyes on the pressurised single-engine market. At the time it looked as if the Cessna P210 Pressurised Centurion would have that segment of the market all to itself. Piper needed an aircraft to counter the Centurion if it was to achieve its long-term goal.

Piston-Powered Predecessors

In 1978 James Edward 'Jim' Griswold left Cessna to become director of engineering at Piper. The company wanted an aircraft able to carry six people, including the pilot, with a low wing and cabin door entry. Looking to the future, the new model had to be capable of forming the basis of a family of aircraft to satisfy different market niches. Griswold was given the task of creating the new design and would oversee it until he left the company in 1984.

The prototype PA-46-300T Malibu (N35646) first flew on November 30, 1979. Although the prototype lacked the cabin pressurisation intended for production aircraft, the Malibu would go on to become only the third with it after the Mooney M22 (the last of which was built in 1970) and P210 Centurion.

The first production PA-46-310P Malibu flew in August 1982, powered by a Continental TSIO-520BE engine of 310hp (230kW), turning a two-blade propeller. Piper announced the Malibu programme that November, with the aircraft receiving its Federal Aviation Administration (FAA) Type Certificate on September 27, 1983. Deliveries started in the last month of that year.

During the late 1980s Continental suffered some quality control issues producing their power plants, leading Piper to seek an alternative for the Malibu. The replacement selected was the Lycoming TIO-540-AE2A of 350hp (261kW), while the opportunity was also taken to increase the aircraft's maximum

take-off weight from 4,118lb to 4,318lb (1,868kg to 1959kg) and install a new electrical system. Most of the weight increase was accounted for by a revised interior installed in the aircraft. After all the changes the aircraft was relaunched as the PA-46-350P Malibu Mirage, which was introduced in October 1988 as the 1989 model. A total of 403 PA-46-310Ps were built before the switch.

However, the new engine had some downsides. Although it was more powerful it did not give the variant any better performance, just burnt more fuel. Range decreased from the Malibu's 1,550nm (2,870km) with reserves to 1,055nm (1,954km) in the Malibu Mirage, although this was subsequently increased by just under a third. In the early 1990s Lycoming engines also began to experience severe problems with their crankshafts, resulting in an Airworthiness Directive that effectively grounded the fleet for a while.

At the heart of the PA-46's problems were the excessive heat and wear on the piston engine generated by the need to not only provide thrust but also power for the cabin pressurisation system. Although the airframe was good, the timing of the troubles was not. In July 1991 Piper Aircraft had entered Chapter 11 bankruptcy protection, in

part due to the 'product liability' cases that had a devastating impact on light aircraft manufacturing in the United States. It was not until July 1995 that the firm re-emerged from Chapter 11, as The New Piper Aircraft, under new ownership. During that year the interior of the Malibu Mirage was revamped, while plans for a new, more powerful member of the family began to be formulated. In September 2006 the company once again became Piper Aircraft.

Turboprop Power

Planning for a turboprop variant started in the mid-1990s, with the aim of creating a Malibu that could carry an additional 500lb (227kg) at higher cruising speeds. Piper wanted a low-cost, high-performance aircraft with a turboprop engine that would appeal to both owner-operators and business flight departments. The Pratt & Whitney Canada PT6A-42A turboprop was selected to power the aircraft, flat-rated to 400shp (298kW) for take-off and 350shp (261kW) maximum continuous in the cruise. This gave rise to the aircraft's original PA-46-400TP designation. The aircraft was announced at the 1997 National Business Aviation Association (NBAA) Convention in

ABOVE • The M500 is the current version of the PA-46-500TP produced by Piper, equipped with Garmin G1000NXi avionics as standard. PIPER

RIGHT • The wing root fillets of the PA-46-500TP contain the extra fuel carried by this version of the Malibu family and help keep its stall speed within certification limits. They are specific to the model. PIPER

ABOVE • *The power from the Pratt & Whitney Canada PT6A was increased for the M600 in comparison to the previous versions of the PA-46, increasing the aircraft's maximum speed.* PIPER

Dallas, Texas, in October, where the company displayed a mockup of the fuselage to potential customers.

The cockpit panel of the PA-46-400TP was designed around the Avidyne Entegra electronic flight information system (EFIS), with three liquid-crystal displays (two primary and one multifunction), the first aircraft in its class to adopt the technology. The EFIS made use of equipment sourced from other companies; Garmin supplied the audio panel, navigation and transponder, S-Tec the flight control system and Meggitt Avionics the electronic instrument displays.

Changes to the basic Malibu airframe included a larger wing with a stronger spar, which featured root fillets to increase area and accommodate more fuel, up to 170 US gal (644lit), 50 US gal (189lit) above that of the Malibu Mirage. The alterations to the wing also keep the aircraft's stalling speed within the 61kts (113km/h) certification limit for single-engined types in the United States, avoiding the need to meet additional crashworthiness

criteria. The area of the horizontal tail surfaces was increased by 37% to enhance longitudinal stability at high cruise speeds, while a new electrically-operated trim tab was installed on the rudder to ease stick forces. Maximum take-off weight had increased to 4,850lb (2,200kg), necessitating a stronger landing gear.

The prototype (N400PT) was created from the airframe of the second Malibu Mirage. It was rolled out on August 13, 1998, and made its maiden flight eight days later. Three further aircraft were built on production tooling for the flight certification test programme, plus a static test airframe. The first to fly (N403MM) took to the air in July 1999, and was used for stability, autopilot and icing trials. It was followed by N402MM on August 27, the first with a production standard interior and external paint finish. Its role in the flight test campaign was to check performance criteria and test the avionics, as well as evaluate the flight into known icing system. Later it became the company's initial demonstrator for the type. The last

of the three, N401MM, first flew in September 1999 and took part in systems and power plant trials, as well as exploring the high-speed range of the flight envelope and its flutter characteristics.

While the additional power of the PA-46-400TP improved performance, more was needed. During the flight test campaign, the PT6A was adjusted to provide 500shp (373kW) for take-off – still less than half its thermodynamic capability – and 400shp (298kW) continuous power. It meant the aircraft could carry more across an expanded flight envelope. The change also meant the designation 'had' to be altered, to PA-46-500TP, which was named the Malibu Meridian. The public got its first chance to inspect the aircraft in October 1999, when the second of the pre-production prototypes was displayed at the NBAA Convention at Atlanta, Georgia.

Deliveries and Upgrades
The first production aircraft (N375RD) flew on June 30, 2000. FAA certification

ABOVE • *The current production standard M500 is equipped with Garmin G1000NXi avionics with three screens. This aircraft has an Aspen EFD1000 standby instrument (on the far left) in case of the primary system failing, which has been replaced by the Garmin GI 275 on later production aircraft.*
PIPER

Piper M500

Wingspan	13.11m (43ft 0in)
Length	9.02m (29ft 7in)
Height	3.44m (11ft 3in)
Max take-off weight	2,310kg (5,092lb)
Max landing weight	2,200kg (4,850lb)
Max zero fuel weight	2,200kg (4,850lb)
Operating empty weight	1,559kg (3,436lb)
Useable fuel	170 US gal (644 lit)
Max cruise speed at 30,000ft	260kts
Ceiling	30,000ft (9,145m)
Range	1,000nm (1,852km) with 45 min reserves
Seating	Up to six, including pilot
Engine	One Pratt & Whitney Canada PT6A-42A flat-rated to 500shp (373kW)

was awarded on September 27 followed by UK Civil Aviation Authority approval on June 21, 2001. The Meridian proved popular, and sales were initially brisk. It was the lowest priced, pressurised, single-engine turboprop on the market, a distinction it held for nearly two decades. Deliveries began in late 2000, when 18 were shipped, followed by 98 the next year as production ramped up.

The original S-Tec Magic 550 autopilot was replaced by the Meggitt Magic 1500 system from mid-2002, starting with the 148th aircraft (N802MM, c/n 4697148). From the end of the same year the maximum take-off weight of the Meridian was increased by about 15%, to 5,092lb (2,310kg). This required some strengthening of the airframe and modifications to the stall strips on the wings, under which vortex generators were added, the same devices also appearing on the lower surfaces of the horizontal tailplanes. The alterations were incorporated in new build examples from the 157th Meridian (N235TW, c/n 4697157) in 2003 and were available to earlier aircraft as a retro kit (known as 767-360). Deliveries in 2002 amounted to only 25 PA-46-500TPs, however, and did not pick up significantly until the late 2000s when they averaged around 45 a year.

Although the Avidyne Entegra EFIS was the standard avionics fit, Piper later offered the Garmin G1000 and GFC700 autopilot as an option, with the first Meridian so equipped delivered in March 2009. The popularity of the integrated Garmin suite resulted in it being adopted as standard for production aircraft built from 2011. The Premier Elegance interior also became an option in October 2012, before becoming the default cabin layout at the start of 2013, with a choice of four colour palettes. By then, Piper was handing

over around 30 Meridians each year, although this dropped to only a dozen by 2016.

The M500

Details of the next iteration of the Meridian were announced by Piper on January 28, 2015. Known as the M500, it was part of a wider overhaul of the PA-46 family that resulted in the creation of the current 'M-Class' family, which includes the M350 (an update of the PA-46-350P) and later the M600. The Malibu Meridian name was no longer used for the M500.

By the time it had been revealed the new variant had already been approved by the FAA, which had updated the Type Certificate on December 14, 2014. Technically the aircraft remains a PA-46-500TP, M500 being the marketing designation for the type when equipped with the 'Garmin G1000/GFC700 Phase III option'.

The M500 had G1000 avionics with a GFC700 autopilot with auto-engage, and enhanced safety features including electronic stability and underspeed protection, coupled go-around, and expanded engagement envelope. Other improvements included digital pressurisation, while the original Aspen EFD1000 standby instrument was retained until replaced by the Garmin GI 275 unit.

The initial M500s were delivered to American operators in January 2015. While authorities in Brazil, Canada and Japan soon approved the M500, Piper had to wait 20 months, until August 16, 2016, for EASA to update the PA-46's

Type Certificate in Europe. By then at least three had been delivered to customers on the continent (although retaining their US 'N-numbers'), with one of (if not the) first going to a Swiss owner based at Wangen-Lachen.

From the 2018 production model the updated Garmin G1000NXi avionics became the factory fit. It benefitted from faster processing, brighter displays of higher resolution, and had enhanced functionality in comparison to the earlier suite. The G1000NXi used a pair of 264mm (10.4in) primary flight displays and a single 315mm (12.4in) multi-function display, which the pilot(s) interface via a GCU 47X keypad.

By the end of 2019 Piper had delivered 87 M500s, but production decreased sharply as the COVID-19 pandemic began to disrupt supply chains. Only seven aircraft were shipped in both 2020 and 2021, but the annual total began to increase again the following year, with eight handed over in the first three quarters. By the end of September 2022, 684 PA-46-500TPs of all versions had been delivered and production continued at Vero Beach, Florida.

Piper began work on the M600 in 2014 as a replacement at the top of its range for the PA-46-500TP Malibu Meridian. The Meridian had been launched in 1997 and was well received, with the 500th handed over to a customer in Florida in September 2015. Piper planned a two-pronged approach to capitalise on its success, refreshing the aircraft as the M500 and creating a more powerful variant, the M600. The aim was to retain the performance of the M500 ✈

at the higher weights planned for the M600.

A New Wing and More Power

Significant changes to the airframe were confined to the wing, which was redesigned with a slightly longer span, thicker roots, greater area, and upturned wingtips. A slight sweepback was also added to the leading edges. The opportunity was also taken to place the main landing gear further out on the wing, improving ground stability over earlier PA-46 versions.

Each wing retained a single fuel tank, but total capacity was increased to 263 US gal (996lit), which was fed to the turboprop via a digital fuel management system. With full tanks the earlier Meridian had 173 US gal (655lit) of fuel. A Garmin GWX70 weather radar was embedded in a pod on the starboard wing, later replaced by the GWX75 (with an option for the higher spec GWX8000).

A higher maximum gross weight was set for the M600, up from the Meridian's 5,092lb (2,310kg), to accommodate the additional fuel. The fuselage was

also reinforced to cope with the higher weights, while greater use was made of bonded structures in comparison to the earlier PA-46 variant.

Power was provided by a Pratt & Whitney Canada PT6A-42A, capable of producing up to 1,029shp (767kW). Although the engine of the M600 was the same as installed in the earlier Meridian, its flat-rating was increased by 100shp (73.5kW) to 600shp (448kW) – with the horsepower of the turboprop providing the digits for the aircraft's designation. While the PT6A is 'overkill' in terms of its unrestricted

ABOVE • *The first Piper M600 (N401MM) flew on May 12, 2014, from its facility at Vero Beach, Florida. It was joined by two further aircraft for the flight test campaign.* PIPER

power output, it is in widespread service and thus has a large and experienced support network, is extremely reliable and has built-in potential to cope with any further weight increase of the airframe. Alternatives to the PT6A are also thin on the ground for designers working at the lighter end of turboprop-powered aircraft spectrum; it is a segment of the market largely bypassed by many of the world's leading engine manufacturers, especially in the west. The PT6A powers nearly all the aircraft in the single-engine turboprop market today. Flat rating the turboprop also reduces wear on components of the engine, increasing its life. In the M600 it would originally turn a four-blade Hartzell constant-speed, reversible propeller.

Cockpit and Cabin

The Garmin G3000 avionics suite was selected for the M600, with two primary flight displays and a single-function display, which allows the pilot to navigate through data via a pair of touchscreen cockpit units. A GFC 700 autopilot was standard, while various information databases (such as FliteCharts and SafeTaxi) were also incorporated.

Interior design is important in the market the M600 was aimed at. While owner-pilots make up a significant proportion of the purchasers of single-engine turboprops and can appreciate the subtilties of the cockpit layout and avionics, most customers will spend the majority of their time in the cabin. It has to match their expectations and lifestyle aspirations.

The M600 was designed to carry six occupants, including a single pilot, typically with a 'club four' (with two seats side-by-side facing to the rear, opposite another pair facing forward) seating arrangement in the cabin. Lightweight, laminated woodwork tables between the seats could

ABOVE • *The M500 can be equipped with a weather radar under the starboard wing. The current standard option is the Garmin GWX 8000.* DAVID WILLIS

RIGHT • *While the M600/SLS also introduced upgrades to the interior and support packages, it was the variant's ability to land automatically should the pilot become incapacitated that was the most noteworthy improvement. The M600/SLS introduced the capability to the single-engine turboprop market.* PIPER

be stowed in the side panels. Each passenger had access to a USB port, an item that became ubiquitous in most business aircraft during the 2000s.

Simon Caldecott, Piper's chief executive officer, contacted Blokx Design of New York to create the furnishings and finishings of the M600's cabin. According to Blokx: "We designed the M600 interior to complement their [Piper's] upgraded performance package and avionics... continuing to step up their game." Customers could choose from Firenze, Mojave, Sequoia, or Geneva premium leather finishes.

Development

Piper completed the maiden flight of the M600 unannounced on May 12, 2014, work on the aircraft having only been revealed to a select few. It publicly revealed the project on April 13, 2015. By then, the original three PA46-500TPs built (N401MM, N402MM and N403MM) had been modified to serve as the M600 flight test aircraft, while static fatigue and test airframes had been constructed to help with certain aspects

of the programme. The three aircraft had accumulated nearly 800 flight hours by the time the M600 was revealed, at which point Piper's dealer network had signed up customers for all the aircraft expected to be completed in the first 12 months of production.

The public first got to inspect the M600 at EAA AirVenture 2015 at Oshkosh in Wisconsin, between July 20 and 26, albeit as a mock-up of the fuselage. At that point, certification and service entry was expected to be achieved in the fourth quarter of the year. This was delayed, however, with Piper announcing that it had decided to incorporate approval for flight into known icing (FIKI) conditions from the outset, rather than adding it as an option later. Service entry was pushed back to the first quarter of 2016 (a target that would subsequently be missed). In addition to working on the anti-icing system, the manufacturer was also optimising the internal wing structure of the aircraft and achieve the guaranteed operating speed of 250kts (463km/h). Two of the three

flight test aircraft had their wings modified as part of this effort.

Type Inspection Authorization (TIA) from the Federal Aviation Administration was announced on March 18, 2015, at which point the three M600s had recorded over 1,440 flight hours. TIA marked the start of the official process of assessing that the aircraft met the criteria for award of its Type Certificate.

Initial Deliveries

From April 5 to 10, 2016, Piper took N401MM out of the flight test campaign to exhibit at the annual Sun 'n' Fun fly-in at Lakeland, Florida - the public debut of a 'real' M600. On May 23 the company began function and reliability testing for the aircraft using N403MM, which was fitted with a representative cabin interior.

Award of the FAA Type Certificate for the M600 was granted on June 16, although without approval for FIKI, which was then expected to be achieved in December 2016. On the plus side, the aircraft had a range 284nm (526km) higher than the stated target, while the true air speed cruise

ABOVE • *The most important structural change for the M600 over the earlier Meridian was the wing, which had a redesigned profile with a swept leading edge and upturned tips. Pilots report that it gives the M600 the feel of 'a big aircraft'.* PIPER

was 24kts (44kph or 27.6mph) higher than the 250kts (463kph) originally announced. In all legal documents the M600 is the PA-46-600TP and was certified as a variant of the wider PA-46 family.

The first M600 delivered (N600BT) was handed over to Jerry and Jack Wardlaw of southern Georgia by the dealer Flightline Group on July 12, 2016. Piper received the production certificate for the aircraft from the FAA on September 1, allowing it to 'sign-off' on completed M600s. Certification in additional countries followed, with Australia (September 20), Mexico (the next day), Canada and Brazil (both in January 2017) among the earlier authorities to accept the M600. The European Aviation Safety Agency (EASA) Type Certificate came on May 19, 2017, albeit still without approval for FIKI. The first 35 M600s were completed without FIKI approval but were eligible for upgrade when the de-icing boots and associated equipment was finally approved. The first European M600 was handed over to a customer in the Czech Republic.

By July 2017 39 M600s had been delivered to private owners and corporations. During that month the fleet was briefly grounded, after an aft wing spar in one aircraft was found to be non-conforming during production. The FAA mandated the inspection of the item in all M600s, and its repair if needed, prior to returning the aircraft to the air, with most of the fleet back in operation by September.

New Levels of Safety

In 2018 Piper offered a premium option package for the M600. It included a Hartzell swept five-blade composite propeller that reduced vibration; Garmin Flight Stream 510 for Bluetooth connectivity; AmSafe seatbelts for the pilot and co-pilot, and 110V AC electrical outlets to re-charge handheld devices in both the cockpit and cabin. Additional avionics and equipment could also be specified by the customer in various pre-bundled packages, including the so-called awareness (with traffic information and reporting systems), weather (with digital updates), and international (replacing some avionics more suited to US owners) options.

By then, Piper had a far more ambitious goal in its sights. Advances in automation presented the possibility of creating a system to recover the aircraft should the pilot become incapacitated.

This had never been incorporated in an aircraft in the class of the M600 before. Piper teamed with Garmin, the producer of the aircraft's avionics, to develop and incorporate the capability in the M600. Known as the HALO Safety System, it made use of Garmin Autoland, which was integrated with the G3000 avionics. Garmin Autoland includes auto-throttle, an emergency descent mode, electronic stability, and protection, SurfaceWatch, SafeTaxi, TerminalTraffic and Flight Stream 510 connectivity – which are collectively known as Autonomi.

It can be engaged automatically or by a passenger and assumes control of the aircraft, communicating with air traffic authorities with details of the new flight route and estimated time of arrival. The system takes account of the length of the runway and orientation, wind, time, fuel range and glide path, and considers weather conditions and terrain along the route. After touch-down the brakes are applied automatically to bring the aircraft to a full stop, after which the engine is shut down.

Piper announced the M600/SLS – standing for Safety, Luxury and Support – on October 30, 2019, as the next iteration of the aircraft. 'Safety' was covered by the HALO system. The previously optional EXP interior package became standard in the M600/SLS, the 'Luxury' component of SLS. 'Support' was provided via the Ultimate Care Program, which covered all scheduled maintenance, as well as hourly and calendar-based inspections for the initial five years of ownership.

Much of the testing of the Garmin Autoland system undertaken in the

M600 took place at Garden City Regional Airport in Kansas, where a demonstration for the FAA occurred on May 5, 2020. The M600/SLS received its Type Certificate 13 days later. Deliveries of the variant began soon after and 36 were delivered in 2020. Handover of the first for a European operator was then expected in the second quarter of 2021. HALO was certified by EASA in April 2021, by when the M600/SLS had demonstrated more than 100 automatic landings.

Recent milestones for the M600 include approval of a Minimum Equipment List (MEL). Announced by Piper on July 25, 2022, MEL outlines the systems and capabilities needed in individual aircraft to permit their use on Part 135 charter operations. It opens up a whole new market for the aircraft. In late 2022 the M600 was also approved for operations from unpaved runways. The capability is built in from the 198th M600 built, with a retro kit available for earlier aircraft. By the start of 2023 around 230 M600s had been registered, of which 206 had been delivered by the end of the third quarter of 2022.

Although production of the M600 is likely to continue for some time to come, Piper continues to work on additional members of the PA-46 family. Although details are sparse, in May 2022 the company registered two PA-46-700TPs as N701PX and N702PX. As of early 2023 the company had released no details of the latest version of the PA-46 range, although the TP suffix appears to indicate the continued use of a turboprop powerplant.

Piper M600 Characteristics	
Wingspan	13.05m (43ft 1in)
Length	9.05m (29ft 8in)
Height	3.44m (11ft 3in)
Max Take-off Weight	2,722kg (6,000lb)
Max Landing Weight	2,631kg (5,800lb)
Max Zero Fuel Weight	2,200kg (4,850lb)
Operating Empty Weight	1,692kg (3,730lb)
Useable Fuel	263 US gal (996lit)
Max cruise speed at 28,000ft	274kts
Ceiling	30,000ft (9,145m) max operating altitude
Range	2,741km (1,480nm)
Seating	Up to six, including pilot
Engine	One Pratt & Whitney Canada PT6A-42A flat-rated to 600shp (448kW)

The M28 – From Cash to Wily Coyote

The PZL Mielec M28 has found favour as a rugged light military transport and maritime surveillance aircraft. Originally conceived in the Soviet Union, its Polish manufacturer and later American owners have continued to refine the basic design, as David Willis details.

I n the late 1960s the Soviet Union required a new light transport to operate from rough airstrips to replace the Antonov An-2 and other types flown by Aeroflot. Antonov used its earlier An-14 as the basis for the An-28 Cash 15-seater, which first flew in September 1969. Two further prototypes of the An-28 were produced at Kyiv in Ukraine and the aircraft was evaluated against the Beriev Be-30 and Czech Let L-410.

The An-28 had a low priority within Antonov, and production was handed over to PZL (Polskie Zakłady Lotnicze) at Mielec in Poland in 1978. It was not until June 22, 1984, that the initial production aircraft flew. An-28 production is usually quoted as 191, of which 157 went to Aeroflot. The exact number built is difficult to pinpoint, as some were only partially completed at the time the Soviet Union was dissolved, while others were finished as later versions by the Polish company.

Bryza

With the main customer for the An-28 unable to afford the aircraft, PZL Mielec sought others who could. In September 1981 it built a prototype of a transport/paradrop version as the M28B1 (SP-PDE). The airframe was later modified as the M28B Bryza TD, with a ramp that slide under the fuselage and with capacity for 17 paratroopers, which was evaluated by the Polish Air

Force from May 1995. Ten production examples were delivered to the service from March 2002.

The Polish Navy also had a requirement for a maritime reconnaissance aircraft, resulting in the An-28RM Bryza 1RM, a prototype (SP-PDC) of which flew in June 1992 and was evaluated by the service from June 1993. Seven production aircraft were delivered between late 1994 and 2001 as M28B1R Bryza 1Rs for 44 BLotM. All eight later had their WSK-Rzeszów TWD-10B engines replaced with PZL-10Ss with five (rather than three) blade propellers. Although it was planned to upgrade them as the Bryza 1RM/Bis for the anti-

submarine role in the early 2000s, only one was completed before the project was abandoned. The fleet had their original ARS-400 surface search radars replaced by the later ARS-800 by mid-2016.

The Polish Navy also receive a single An-28 originally intended for the electronic intelligence gathering role as the Bryza 2RF, although it served as a transport devoid of its mission equipment. Two Bryza 1TD transports were also delivered to the navy (while another pair were transferred from the air force in 2002). The only other version flown by the service is the An-28E Bryza 1E pollution control

ABOVE • *Wearing the colours of 304 Squadron, Polish Navy Bryza 1R 1017 has the PZL-10S engines and Hartzell five-blade propellers retrofitted to the fleet. The Polish Navy unit that operates the aircraft traces its ancestry back to the RAF squadron.* DAVID WILLIS

ABOVE • *The PZL Mielec M28 programme now belongs to Lockheed Martin following the company's purchase of Sikorsky Aircraft.*
LOCKHEED MARTIN

aircraft, equipped with the Swedish Space Corporation MSS-5000 maritime surveillance system.

The second major variant for the Polish Air Force, the M28B/PT was powered by Pratt & Whitney Canada PT6A-65B turboprops rather than the TWD-10S. They also had night-vision goggle-compatible Rockwell Collins digital avionics. Two were delivered by December 2006, followed by further orders for three and 12, although the last four were cancelled.

The Skytruck

The M28 Skytruck was developed to compete on the export market. The basic airframe was powered by PT6A-65B turboprops, turning Hartzell five-blade propellers, and fitted with Bendix-King Gold Crown avionics, an RDR-2000 digital weather radar and other equipment. Work on the prototype (SP-PDF) began in early 1991 and the aircraft first flew on July 24, 1993. A temporary Polish certificate was awarded for the first production variant in March 1994 and full approval granted in March 1996, permitting a maximum take-off weight of 7,000kg (15,432lb), which was later increased to 7,500kg (16,534lb) in the M28 02-W on April 18, 2002. Stretched variants were

considered as the 03 and 04 before work on them was abandoned. The M28 05 became the baseline production model in 1999, receiving its Federal Aviation Administration (FAA) Type Certificate on March 19, 2004.

Early Customers

Latina de Aviación of Colombia became the initial customer to receive an M28 when it took delivery of the second built as HK-4066X in January 1996. At the time 12 had been ordered, including six M28 02s for the Venezuelan National Guard, which received its first in December 1996 and subsequently doubled its commitment the following year. Venezuela became a major customer for the M28 as the Army also ordered 12, which were delivered between April 2000 and the end of the following year.

Nepal became the next operator of the M28, with single examples of the 05 received in November 2002 and October 2003. PZL Mielec expected further examples to be ordered by the mountainous kingdom, but had to wait until March 2019, when two M28 05s were purchased using US Foreign Military Financing (FMF). They were officially handed over on December 18, 2019. On February 3, 2023, PZL Mielec

was awarded a $30m FMF deal for another pair, plus a support package, for Nepal. The latest aircraft will be delivered by April 2025.

Vietnam wanted eight to ten M28s equipped for maritime surveillance and border patrol. An initial two M28 05s were ordered in late October 2003 and delivered in December 2004 as light transports, with the intention of installing mission equipment later. The plans changed, however, with Vietnam instead ordering the Airbus (CASA) 212 to fulfil its maritime requirement.

Indonesia became the third Asian operator for the M28, in late 2003. Four M28 05PIs were purchased for the Polisi Udara (national police) and delivered in pairs in October and December 2004. At the same time, Indonesia expressed an interest for three transports and seven for maritime patrol for its Navy. Although a contract for the ten was signed on August 18, 2005, it was later cancelled.

Combat Coyote

In March 2007, Sikorsky Aircraft acquired PZL Mielec. Although its emphasis for the Polish company was on the production of aerostructures and the S-70i International Black Hawk, promotion of the M28 continued. ✈

In late 2008 the Sierra Nevada Corporation (SNC) ordered M28 05s on behalf of the US Air Force Special Operations Command (AFSOC) for the Combat Coyote programme. A total of 17 were eventually delivered, while another (registration N305ST) served with the SNC subsidiary Straight Flight Nevada Commercial Leasing as a testbed. The Mission Design Series C-145A was allocated on May 16, 2012, and the popular name Alfa adopted, although rarely used. Around the same time the fleet began to wear military identities rather than the N-numbers originally carried.

The C-145A entered service with the 318th Special Operations Squadron (SOS), a component of the 27th Special Operations Wing (SOW) at Cannon Air Force Base, New Mexico. Three aircraft were deployed to Afghanistan for the first time on March 7, 2011, operating in the 'village stability' role, but one was destroyed in an accident there on December 18, 2011. The C-145A fleet was also active in Africa, operating from airfields in the Central African Republic, the Democratic Republic of Congo, South Sudan, and Uganda, in support of African Union operations against the Lord's Resistance Army. C-145As also flew missions in Central America.

The 318th SOS withdrew the C-145A on March 28, 2013, transferring its last to the 6th SOS at Duke Field, Florida. In May 2013, the aircraft also joined the 711th SOS. Both units undertook the Aviation Foreign Internal Defense mission, training allied forces. The majority were retired between May 28 and August 28, 2015, when nine were sent for storage at Davis-Monthan Air Force Base, Arizona, while the last two delivered passed to the Arizona Department of Public Safety. Five C-145As were retained by the 6th SOS until it was inactivated on October 6, 2022, leaving the 711th SOS to fly the aircraft. The last four C-145As were retired at Duke Field on December 15, 2022.

Latest Operators

Two M28 05s were delivered to the Royal Jordanian Air Force in December 2014 and December 2015, entering service with No.3 Squadron at Amman-Marka. By then, Lockheed Martin had purchased Sikorsky. Both Jordanian M28s were modified in turn by SNC at Centennial, Colorado, spending 12 months there from August 2016 and June 2018, respectively, returning

ABOVE • *Three of the last C-145As in US Air Force service taxiing at Duke Field, Florida, on December 15, 2022. In its last years in service the aircraft was used exclusively in the Aviation Foreign Internal Defense role.* US AIR FORCE/SENIOR AIRMAN DYLAN GENTILE

PZL Mielec M28 05

Wingspan	22.06m (72ft 4in)
Length	13.10m (42ft 11in)
Height	4.90m (16ft 1in)
Max take-off weight	7,500kg (16,534lb)
Max landing weight	7,500kg (16,534lb)
Max zero fuel weight	6,600kg (14,550lb)
Operating empty weight	4,398kg (9,695lb) configured for passengers
Useable fuel	592 US gal (2,240lit)
Cruise speed	145kts (270kph) econ cruising speed at FL984
Ceiling	25,000ft (7,620m) at MTOW
Seating	Up to 19 passengers, plus two pilots
Range	855nm (1,583km) at FL100 with max fuel and 45 min reserves
Engine	Two Pratt & Whitney Canada PT6A-65B of 1,100shp (820kW)

with some additional aerials on their airframes. From November 2017, PD Air Operation, part of the German private defence contractor PD Sicherheit, received the first of three M28 05s. The company uses them to support German special forces and for parachute training.

In addition to the new M28s shipped by Lockheed Martin, two operators have received surplus C-145As from the US supplied under the Excess Defense Article programme. Two went to the Estonian Air Force in March and June 2019 after overhaul at Centennial, while Kenyan Air Force crews trained on the aircraft from September 2019 at Hurlburt Field, Florida, before it received three

in April and June 2021, and February 2022.

SNC also promoted a variant known as the MC-145B Wily Coyote to meet the US Special Operations Command's (USSOCOM) Armed Overwatch requirement, designed to provide intelligence surveillance and reconnaissance, and air support, to troops on the ground. The MC-145B has wing pylons, a retractable sensor, additional fuel tanks and internal weapons launchers. Although demonstrated to USSOCOM at Eglin Air Force Base, Florida, in late 2021, the AT-802U Sky Warden offered by L3Harris Technologies was selected instead.